Life, lo ... ~~~~~~ up

Life, love and washing up

The musings of a Liverpool columnist

David Charters

Life, love and washing up
David Charters

Cartoons by Ivan Frontani

First published in 2006 by
Palatine Books,
Carnegie House,
Chatsworth Road
Lancaster LA1 4SL
www.palatinebooks.com

ISBN 10: 1-874181-38-1
ISBN 13: 978-1-874181-38-5

British Library Cataloguing-in-Publication data
A catalogue record for this book is available from the British Library

Designed, typeset and originated by Carnegie Book Production
www.carnegiebookproduction.com

Printed and bound in Great Britain by Alden Press, Whitney, UK

Preface

I have never been greatly impressed by the big events of the world; they usually don't affect us much But if your braces snap when you are running for the bus, then you're in real trouble. Behind nearly everything I write is an understanding that failure is more interesting than success, and that you can only be happy if you laugh at yourself. When I was very young and looked in the mirror, I realised that I would have very little difficulty achieving that ambition. Thinking that you're important is the biggest obstacle to happiness, and in writing my columns I have always kept that in mind. I do hope that you have as much fun reading my musings as I have had writing them.

David Charters
2006

These columns were first published in the *Liverpool Daily Post*

David Charters has been a journalist on Merseyside for more than 40 years, working for national, regional and local papers. For the past 18 years, he has worked for the *Liverpool Daily Post*. During this time he has been a reporter, news editor and feature writer, winning several awards on the way, but it is for his weekly column that he is best known.

This book is dedicated to my wife Alison and my son Cameron

James Bond, Y-fronts
and scrambled egg

"Do you think that I would make a good Bond girl?" asked my wife in the falling gloom of evening, when we were walking home from church, hand in hand under the weeping trees, passing by the leaves sighing slowly in their russet piles.

"By jove," I replied, pausing surreptitiously to decapitate one of the more defiant spots frolicking on the upper thigh of my left leg. "You certainly have all the right attributes, but I don't think Ian Fleming set many of his hero's adventures in suburban Birkenhead.

"Did he not favour more exotic locations, where beautiful people with oodles of money jet-ski, and drinks are served with slices of lemon in fluted glasses? Maybe we could further your ambition by moving to Scunthorpe."

As we advanced along the pavement, joined by other members of the congregation, eager to discuss the priest's thought-provoking homily on respecting the true values in life, a picture began to loom before me of my wife: her fair flesh lightly goosepimpled by the autumnal breeze, swaying to the corner shop for a bag of pippins in her stiletto-heeled shoes, a jewelled dagger poking from the belt of her briefest bikini.

"Do you think, I would make a good James Bond?" I asked her, to the surprise of our companions, who were still deeply enmeshed in the theological implications of, "Render unto Caesar the things which are Caesar's and unto God the things that are God's".

"No," she said, briskly, leaving little room for doubt. "You are not brave, you are not dashing, you are not suave, you can't drive, and more than all those things, you don't care if your red wine is stirred or shaken, as long as it says 14% on the label; and, through the

corner of my eye, I have just spotted you itching yourself in a very un-Bondish manner."

That said we all returned to Matthew 21/22, before switching to some juicy nuggets of gossip of that familiar sort which helps to lubricate life. But I knew what lay behind my wife's thinking. For the past week or so the newspapers and magazines have been filled with pictures of Daniel Craig, the actor, who spent part of his childhood in Wirral and has been chosen as the next 007.

I have to admit here that my wife has the most girlish crush on this chap, breathing warmly and passionately on his photographs, which now adorn every spare space in the house.

"Oh Danny boy, the pipes, the pipes are calling . . . 'tis you, 'tis you must go and I must bide. But come ye back when summer's in the meadow . . ." she trills every time Craig's blue eyes stare radiantly from the television screen and he smiles at her, cool as the tinkle of an ice cube in crystal glass.

"Isn't he a dreamboat?" she says, and her imagination floats away, higher and higher, beyond the Tranmere oil terminal, or even the Seaforth dock complex, to some distant paradise of soft melody, where perfectly tailored suits cover lovingly sculpted bodies and everyone has an even sun tan and a private yacht bobbing on the sparkling waters of the harbour.

It was during such a reverie the other day that I entered the kitchen through the backdoor in my elastic-sided, tartan slippers and poplinette pyjamas, having just unpegged from the washing line four pairs of Y-fronts, three string-vests and my bed-socks.

"The name is Charters, David Charters," I said, with a venturesome stab at satire. Unfortunately, however, my lead foot chanced upon a strip of potato peel lurking on the tiles, causing me to measure my length between the kitchen sink and the fridge. Now, 007 hardly ever falls down and when he does, it is done with supreme elegance.

Has anyone heard a lavatory flushing near James Bond?

But how do we cope with this business of being cool? Some have it and others do not. I think, increasingly, as I enter the creak of mature years that it doesn't really matter much, just be yourself, wear your baggy cardigan with the holes in the elbows and laugh at the consequences.

I have seen enough of the gods down here to know that flawed people are almost always better company and, to use an old-fashioned word, which says a lot, are 'nicer'. Your judgement sharpens, your wisdom deepens and your humour broadens as a result of failure, not success.

Of course, it has to be admitted that I feel the tiniest twinge of envy whenever James Bond sweeps into view, suave as they come with every hair in place. After all he can quicken the pulse of my wife by merely raising an eyebrow. Sadly, however, co-ordination has never been my strong point and I find it very difficult to arch an eyebrow without kicking a leg at the same time, which has made hayfever a particular torment for me and those in the immediate vicinity.

"But you are very good in some ways," said my wife, peeling herself off Bond's photograph. "You might not be a dreamboat, but, by jingo, you can scramble an egg."

〰

"This will certainly see me out"

During a life darkened by many sorrows but decorated by the ever-glowing light of her children's rare triumphs, my late mother received presents on her birthday or at Christmas with a sly little smile that spoke from the grey of her eyes about the silliness of it all.

"Ochh noo, you shouldn't have bothered," she would say in her Scottish accent, which had clung to her like the paint on a kirk door for more than 70 years in England.

And then, surrounded by the family, she would rip the wrapping paper and feel the texture of a chunky brown cardigan or some other heavy-duty item, before adding, "Well, this will certainly see me out".

Her observations would be exactly the same whether there sat on her lap a cardigan, a kettle, or an extra-large box of chocolates.

In later years, when the prophecy was reaching for its stark, cold truth, her voice still carried the same tone, that bleakly humorous recognition of the inevitable.

It was this essentially Scottish mood which led her to tell one of the best black jokes I have ever heard, as we left the municipal cemetery, having buried one of her oldest friends. The air was misted and damp and the turf squelched underfoot as it always does at funerals. Plastic grass lay on the mud at the foot of the holes, where, one after the other, the wind-flushed priests had stood in their robes, books in hand, while the ink ran on the labels tied to the flowers.

"You know," she said, looking around her, "it hardly seems worth the trouble of going home."

My mother was not in the least hard-up or particularly pessimistic by nature, but she had this attitude, held in common with many of her generation, that you should look after the money throughout your days. There was very little point buying something "ridiculously dear" too late in the show, but there was reassurance to be found in sensible, inexpensive articles, which would see you out.

A jar of crystallised fruits in the pantry wouldn't be of much use once you were gone and what would you do with a silver spoon if you had no tea to stir? On the other hand, a fluff-clad hot water bottle or a nice knee-rug would be most welcome.

Sometimes, very late at night when everyone else is sleeping, I sense such worries breeding in my thoughts.

As teenagers growing up after the war, my generation imagined that life was studded by certainties. You would leave school with the qualifications necessary to do this or that, then you'd have a few fancy years to dance and sing and hop and drink and love and dream, before meeting the right girl/boy and settling down to have children in a stout brick house. Later, you would retire with your solid pension to a reassuring hearth for your rocking-chair years, visited from time to time by grandchildren, who would tolerate your rambling reminiscences with affectionate sighs and raised eyes.

But something often happens to interrupt the anticipated flow of events. There are illnesses, wars and economic slumps to ambush you along the way, as well as the self-inflicted problems of drink, drugs, love affairs, gambling and unwise investments, which might bedevil you.

On the day, I bought by first suit from Montagu Burton for six pounds seventeen shillings and sixpence (£6.87), I looked at the dark blue, sombre, clerical weave and wondered, in the style of my mother, if it would serve for my funeral as well.

But what would happen in between? It was the mid 1960s and many of the brilliant social commentators, the great prophets, the philosophers and inventors, were predicting that in the future life would be much easier.

Robots and computers would sweep into the work-place and replace people, affording us leisure to develop our potential in the arts or sport. It is true that heavy manual jobs, such as mining and shipbuilding, have almost disappeared, but new occupations, usually connected with commerce, advertising, IT, business consultancies and other fringe activities, have rolled along in their wake.

So hulking, straddle-limbed lads, obviously designed for spud-howking, are now crammed into soulless, air-conditioned halls, phoning people at their homes, hoping to persuade them to join some money-spinning scheme or other.

Forty years on from the utopian forecasts, people are working harder than ever, barely daring to leave their desks, lest they should be judged to have fallen short of the corporate ideal.

The technological revolution has added hugely to our work-loads. Daily, in an unending gush of electronic incontinence, I get emails from strangers wishing to tell me about things in which I have not the slightest interest.

One rather venturesome correspondent hopes that I will try Viagra while another tempts me with brassieres cupped to the special needs of the individual figure. But have these bras the strength to see me out? We all need support.

Naked power

Smart young men do not wear ties these days as they clamber up the buttered rungs of life. To enter the fray tieless is to tell everyone that you are energetic, thrusting and hungry for power.

The naked neck has become a symbol of ambition in today's thrilling world.

Some of my senior colleagues have been seen, in broad daylight, during the working day, standing as bold as you like in public places, wearing shirts open at the top button

I even spotted one young fella, clearly primed to shoot up the promotional ladder like a freshly released champagne cork, surreptitiously undoing his second top button, before striding the corridor towards the canteen queue for cups of Earl Grey tea. Several adventurous tufts of hair nosed through the gap, suggesting that he wasn't wearing a vest. That, to me, was the more serious lapse in decorum.

Briefly I thought of telling him that the British Empire was built and served by men who wore vests, but decided that such information was unlikely to leave a deep impression on a chap in elastic-sided shoes.

The message, though, was obvious enough. If you want to get on don't wear a tie.

So it was in a renascent spirit that I swooshed into the office the next morning in an open-necked shirt, striped in colours vivid enough to speak confidently of my new thrust. I felt young again like a fresh shaver staring into the mirror of opportunity.

But colleagues stared at me in bewilderment mixed with horror. Jowls wobbled, lips trembled and fingers pointed. "Where is it?" they said, one to the other. "Where has it gone?" I began to sense some alarm about this apparent deficiency in my head region.

Grim possibilities sprang into consideration. Had one of my eyes dropped on the pavement? Had an ear slipped its perch? Had my nose shrunk on the train journey in?

I need not have worried. They all started laughing and their observations boiled down to this – very trendy but not really you.

In my day, young men didn't advance unless a tie, preferably in a sensibly dark colour, dangled from their white collars. Unreliable and rakish types, like poets, artists, jugglers and unicyclists, repertory actors, bookies, explorers and insect-collectors, might be permitted droopy bow-ties; but the rest of us were required to fasten our top buttons around the Adam's apple in a grip worthy of the Boston strangler.

And then there was the morning ritual at front-doors when wives and mothers adjusted the knots on the ties of their men folk to an angle and size suited to career advancement.

Our ties were a statement. Manual workers, except foremen and supervisors, didn't wear them at all during the week, though they would have one for the church and another for stepping out with the wife or sweetheart.

But everyone in clerical occupations from the office boy to the managing director wore a tie. White collar jobs were judged to be middle-class with all the special standards of dress that went with that.

In such a society, those who didn't wear ties were thought to be ill-equipped for their duties, like an undertaker without his tape measure or a gigolo reporting for duty without a peppermint lozenge.

Of course, ties could mean something more specific. Golf club and tennis clubs had their own ties as did the armed services. Certain types of men liked to wear their old school ties and on occasion unscrupulous snobs tried to pass themselves off as products of expensive public schools.

It is perhaps noting at this point that the cravat has always been regarded with suspicion. The rotter in old-fashioned plays invariably wore a loud cravat and spoke in an accent that was just a little too polished.

Life, love and washing up

Anyway, there was a time when much could be learned from a chap's neckwear. My wife, however, tells me that the curves and creases on the bottom are the new way of quickly assessing a person's potential.

A few weeks ago I told you of how I bought her The People's Friend every week so that she could read dreamy and innocent tales of romance in the manse and trysts in the mists. Given the opportunity, however, she sneaks off in pursuit of raunchier material.

And a few weeks ago I saw her with a glossy magazine, which featured a psychic called Sam Amos who has been "reading bottoms" for the past four years to earn a crust. Rears can tell us a lot about our temperaments, he opines.

My wife, who describes her bottom as "pert", has "an outgoing personality" which is occasionally punctured by her "fiery nature".

"Spot on," I said, wondering if there could possibly be any valid scientific base for such an accurate appraisal. I, however, am not allowing my cheeks to come under such close scrutiny, believing that everything can be discovered from the tie which I am wearing again.

It is blue and black and a little frayed around the edges.

Begging the question

The old beggar's drink of preference is red biddy and his normally blurry eyes, which often have difficulty focusing on the advance of a double-decked bus, can alight with unexpected clarity on the small print in the corner of the bottle's label. This, of course, is devoted to the alcohol content.

Others in the wine store may mull over the acidity in the soil of the region where the grapes were grown, but the beggar's pale lips smile through his stained stubble when he sees the all-important 17% alc/vol. "That should do it," he whispers.

Once, an assistant behind the counter had asked him whether he favoured old or new world wines.

Smoke rose in thickening twists from the cigarette which the tramp had rolled from dog-ends left on the pavement. "Out-of-this-world wines please me most," he replied, after a pause shaved to perfection.

But one shouldn't jump to the conclusion that he is a snob in such matters; too proud to sully his tongue with a glug or two of one of

the bellow-and-plunder lagers supped by the young, though the man himself is not inclined to either activity.

In fact, he could be said to have a catholic taste in drink, ceaselessly excited by his oceanic thirst. If you give him body splash for Christmas, anticipate sweet breath rather than an alluring aroma under the anorak.

Anyway, of late he has been operating from the railway station instead of his old perch on the pub wall,

Life, love and washing up

where he would sit waiting for people whose natural generosity had been enhanced by an agreeable drink.

This is a canny business move, adding credibility to his claim that any money you give him will be promptly spent on the fare to his next job interview. I would guess that he has been between jobs for about 30 years.

Often in the past, I have him given money, but he caught me by surprise on the platform, where the grey of the drizzle was seeping deep into my mood.

"No," I said in a sudden, cold unfriendly voice before he had finished his question. Almost immediately I felt guilty and several other commuters looked at me with questioning faces.

It is always difficult for a middle-class chap of liberal persuasion to know what to do when confronted by a vagrant in need of a drink, particularly if you are on nodding terms yourself with that thirst which can never be satisfied.

Traditionally, the plight of the tramps, the deranged, the crippled, misfits, the dream-seekers and those who just want to escape the modern world, has attracted the pity of poets, politicians and balladeers.

But they speak of romanticised figures; minstrels of freedom's road striding towards the sun – briar pipe clasped in the teeth, possessions bundled in a spotted handkerchief, a faithful hound padding along behind and a pencil and jotter in hand in case a thought worthy of posterity should come parachuting into mind.

But we cannot be sure that the wino, crouching in a doorway in his great coat, will receive a spiritual fillip from a professor of sociology, equipped with sparse whiskers, a palm-top computer, a compassionate brow and a prominent Adam's apple, singing *We Shall Overcome* in a trembling falsetto.

In my youth, we were much given to strumming guitars and singing songs about the downtrodden, such as *There But For Fortune* and *The Streets Of London*. We also had a strong repertoire of songs about the evils of slavery, which we would unleash at church socials and at birthday parties in old folk's homes, where the general infirmity of the audience, many of whom were amputees, prevented us being pelted with rock buns.

Broadly speaking it has always been true that songs, hymns and poems about the poor and the dying will find an appreciative audience among well-heeled liberals enjoying robust health. In this way, coal dust is breathed by people with clean lungs.

But if you listen to Johnny Cash, who died earlier this month, you will hear his truth and experience in a voice so deep and yearning that it can surely squeeze the souls of the dead.

And so we come to John Lennon's Imagine which was last week the subject of a 90-minute documentary on BBC TV's Arena, generally celebrating the song's simple message. There's nothing wrong with that.

"Imagine no possessions, I wonder if you can," is a challenging sentiment, though the tramp in the doorway may judge it differently to the idealistic student of lyrics.

However, once politicians were almost as eager as the folk singers to identify with the crushed and dispossessed. Remember those great rallies at which orators with cracked voices would pluck out fine words and dedicate them to the poor.

Now we are in the party conference season again. But you won't be hearing much about poverty. In a society dominated by celebrity, the important thing is to look fashionable and to smell expensive.

This is not a good time for beggars.

⌇

J-Lo and the Fuehrer's wind

After she had the house re-carpeted in the shades of autumnal brown, my wife ordered me out of the bathroom, where I used to enjoy applying talcum powder to my feet, to help them slide more easily into their socks.

"You make far too much mess," she said sharply, showing scant consideration for the deftness of touch needed by a chap when manoeuvring the holes in the cap to release exactly the right amount of powder, while simultaneously patting the container's bottom in a teasing manner.

Instead, I have been exiled to the garden. Here, I must sit on a paving-stone while sprinkling my toes. To slow the ground's cold advance into my soles, which suffer from a peculiar sensitivity to changes in temperature, I lay down a newspaper.

On Monday morning, while spraying with unusual vigour to overcome my feet's residual dampness, my eyes were buttoned to an article by Germaine Greer, in which she listed the qualities required of the male nude.

"The male human is beautiful," she wrote encouragingly, before adding, "when his cheeks are still smooth, his body hairless, his head full-maned, his eyes clear, his manner shy and his belly flat."

Well, I am accustomed to performing rather sluggishly in such appraisals, but this time I failed on every count.

Anyway, I decided to read the rest of the article on the way to work. So I folded up the broadsheets and slipped them into my work bag.

As it happened the train was heaving with impatient commuters. I found myself wedged between an aspiring rap star in a woolly hat, who was jerking enthusiastically to the rhythms of his personal-stereo, and a large woman in a fashionable tartan muffler, who was adjusting the safety-pin on the bandage which contained the fluid bubbling under her right knee-cap.

In these uncomfortable circumstances, I began tugging the paper out of the bag perched on my lap. It was then that Lady Luck struck and the train accelerated rapidly, causing us all to lurch forward.

In the momentary confusion the paper unfolded, releasing a blizzard of talcum powder which landed with an uncanny concentration on the thigh region of the pinstriped gentleman sitting opposite.

"Prevents sweaty feet," I volunteered, by way of explanation. He glowered and later I was to wonder whether there had been insufficient room for him to unleash a right uppercut to my chin.

If he had been a more receptive chap, I might have told him how the human is unique in the animal kingdom for being ashamed of his/her own smells. Dogs, for example, not only like their own odours, but are sexually thrilled by those of other creatures.

My old dog was a positive Casanova of the cowpats.

And so we come to poor old Adolf Hitler, who was troubled by poor wind retention throughout his adult life. This, I believe, explains why he was at his best when addressing mass rallies in the open-air, rather than intimate one-to-one meetings with people in windowless rooms.

Some of you may remember the greenish pallor of Prime Minister Neville Chamberlain when he returned to Britain after his infamous 'peace in our time' meeting with Hitler.

"I am afraid the Fuehrer has been on the barley and cabbage soup again," his secretary would confide, as she greeted the parades of hapless generals queuing outside his bunker with reports of new defeats.

Contemporaries remarked on how even the ice-gripped hell of the Eastern Front held no fears for decorated veterans, once they had dwelt for a few seconds in the proximity of their glorious leader.

It has even been suggested that cabbage and barley soup was the fuel used in a proto-type of the V1 rockets, launched with such fearful effect against south east England in June 1944.

Polite society expects men and women to drown their natural smells in sprays, powders and perfumes.

At the weekend, I caught my wife rubbing her wrist with the page of a magazine, which had been impregnated with a new scent being produced by a perfume manufacturer, already anticipating the whirr of the Christmas tills.

Of more interest to me was an item inside the same magazine, which reported that a Jennifer Lopez, described as a singer, had insured her bottom for one billion dollars.

"What against?" I asked my wife. "Is she particularly accident prone in that area? Has she insured it against loss or storm damage? Is her bottom's coverage fully comprehensive or merely third party, fire and theft? Has she been seen dallying with a bacon slicer? If, God forbid, one buttock was damaged, would she be entitled to half a billion dollars in compensation? We should be told.

My wife was also baffled by these questions.

And yet, despite Germaine Greer's observations on male beauty, the idea of insuring my own bottom skipped briefly into morning thoughts.

"Baggy trousers should provide all the coverage your bottom needs," my wife scolded.

↬

Dads and lads

Again I could feel the warm clutch of my late father's hand.

Then, on some fog-gripped afternoon in the late 1950s, he had led me, snaking, through the thundering feet of a beery, gravy-breathed mass of grumbling, steaming men, making their way across the streets like a great unstoppable herd, on their way to the turn-stiles under the great towering stand, where I stood and trembled, bare-kneed, while the bronchial roar within revved and faded and revved again like an engine in a garage.

Click, click, clatter, clatter repeated the rattles and occasionally there would be a lone voice, cutting the air like a prayer in the dusk. "Come on you blue boys."

Now, all these years later, I was walking along on what some said would be the last sunny Saturday of the autumn. And the fingers in my hand belonged to my seven-year-old son. But the sudden rush of tingling blood across the wrist was the same. For the hand which squeezed the fingers had joined the generations.

Of course, passing time does not provide an exact mirror. There were differences. We weren't even in the same place. I had been taken to Everton's Goodison Park, where black priests, their faces mapped in veins, sat in rows at the back of the stand nipping from their hip-flasks. Down below Davy Hickson, blond god to thousands of pale boys, tried to answer their prayers every time he leapt high in a blitz of flying turf to head the heavy leather ball towards that earthly heaven known as the goal – or the 'onion bag', as reporters on local rags would call it in moments of poetic fancy.

"Ah Davy, Davy, if they was all like you, we'd be champions of the world," wheezed the man behind me through the almost impenetrable smoke of his third Woodbine.

But that was dear old Goodison. We were now at Prenton Park, home of Second Division Tranmere Rovers, and the player attracting the attention of the man behind us was Mickey Mellon, the gloriously named midfield 'general'.

"Do something," bellowed the voice, as Mellon tussled with Oldham Athletic's legendary 'playmaker', John Eyre, near the touch-line. As an instruction, this seemed to lack the finesse of the old masters, who would satisfy themselves with a deceptively simple, "lamp the b . . . d".

What was Mellon to do? Compose a concerto, whip a soufflé or open a boutique? In the event he lost the ball. Arguments then broke out around us about the merits of the young man, who happened to be the centre-fold picture in that day's programme.

Few people have been the subject of so much controversy since the brilliant Isaac Newton observed that the trajectory of an apple from a tree tends to be down rather than up, which came as a huge relief to the birds.

Some enthusiasts felt that Mellon combined the skills of George Best with the temperament of Bobby Charlton and the vision of Pele. Others, of a more embittered nature, felt that his replacement with a tub of lard would have been good for the team's morale.

My son, though, was an instant Mellonite. "I would like to see them do better," he whispered, glowering at the seated critics. "I think Mickey's great."

And the colour photograph of the player from the club's excellent programme is now one of his most prized possessions.

Well, professional football has always been like that. You have your heroes and you have your villains and the camps divide with the same fervour that splits religious sects.

For many years I followed Everton home and away, suffering the joys and miseries as my bank balance shrank like a stripper's drawers. But when my wife was pregnant, I stopped going, so that I could devote my weekends to domestic duties.

And I didn't miss the matches as much as I expected. The outrageous vanity and arrogance of Premiership players, their wage demands, the endless flow of foreign mercenaries, the smirking spivs brokering deals; the painted, pouting, grasping celebrity girls seeking out the stars in fashionable night-spots, the flash suits and the speculation about injuries and transfers, began to bore me.

But sometimes in the garden I would hear an appreciative rumble break from Prenton Park. Maybe, I thought, the time has come to take my boy to Tranmere Rovers, as I had been taken to Everton.

So we bought dad and lad tickets for the match – £16 for me and £4 for him. It was a perfect day for football, crisp and clear with only the slightest breeze.

Perhaps, there wasn't the surging herd that I remember from my own childhood, but the sprinkling of spectators grew steadily. At one point we were three abreast on the pavement!

Oldham scored first. "Trrran-meah", chorused the soprano children in scornful reply. In the second half the Rovers pushed on bravely, scoring twice to clinch the win.

My son jumped for joy. "Imagine, my first match and we won," he said. "Mickey's the man. We must come again."

～

Astride the border

Times such as these, when normally peaceable young men chalk their cheeks harlequin-white and then cross them in the crimson of St George's veins, present problems of diplomacy, faith and emotion for that most miscast of all creatures skulking these shores, the Anglo Scot.

And let me tell you that is very different being from a real Scot, who rose in his own land, squelching the same peat bog as his forebears, knowing his place in the world.

You see, we Anglo Scots are thrust into a mire of indecision whenever news breaks of a great English triumph. To be sure, there have been few enough to give us much practice in the recent past; but now we have to contend with this defeat of the mighty Australians in the Rugby World Cup Final. What should we do?

If our own boys thrashed Fiji at shove ha'penny, humiliated the islanders of Tristan da Cunha in a ill-tempered contest of hunt-the-thimble or sneaked an away draw against Papua New Guinea in the annual frisbee-throwing, pancake-tossing and balloon-popping games, we would know exactly what to do. We would go mad, quite delirious in nationalistic joy. The festivities would last for months; with the dancing of reels, the eating of haggis and the growing of oats. Our knobbled knees would be exposed to the winter's chill in kilts stitched in Taiwan and finally we would recite chunks from the poems of Rabbi Burns, rrrrrrolling our Rs like crazed preachers.

But what should we do now that England has won a major tournament in a flawless manner, which does so much credit to all involved?

Should we look at them straight, through our whisky-fumed eyes, webbed with veins, and say, "I am so pleased for you, old chap, you were all wonderful. Would you care to come round for a wee dram and a slice of Dundee cake?"

Should we pretend that we were English all along and simply slip into the celebrations singing, *Swing Low Sweet Chariot* in a Home Counties' accent.

Or should we tell the truth?

As Anglo Scots, we cover our ambiguity by responding to the great sporting contests with a patriotic fervour that you would rarely find in the home-grown Scot, who has so often been drained of his romantic juices by the squeeze of unhappy circumstance.

Rod Stewart, the Cockney-speaking singer and Scotland's most ardent football fan is the prime example of this.

For down here we all believe that our own grrrrreat, great, great, great ... 'grandfaither' was the man chosen by Robert the Bruce himself to lead the Highland charge, which left pretty boy Edward II's army bleeding in the glorious mud of Bannockburn.

"Look that's my great ... grandfaither Hamish," you say, pointing at a flame-haired maniac with a claymore charging out of a tartan-fringed shortbread tin, with a sell-by date of 1314, that nobody north of the border would ever allow in the house. "You can spot the family likeness at once."

Sadly, we were to come a poor second at Culloden in 1746, the last major battle to be fought in Britain. "Och aye, the noo, the Sassenachs took the initiative from the first whistle, leaving our brave, wee men a disorganised rabble with heather seeds in their beards and thistles in their thighs," as I have explained to bewildered companions in the pub.

From this disaster, however, emerged a certain style of Scottish genius. We transformed the absurd, flabby, toad-chinned, Roman-mannered, Italian-speaking Charles Edward Stuart into the glamorous Bonnie Prince Charlie, who dressed up as the maid of Flora MacDonald, so he could be rowed to Portree, safety and legend.

Almost 200 years later, when I was

Life, love and washing up

born, the Scots had hit on another idea. Defeated on the field of battle, they decided to conquer England by other means. In this they were more successful.

Down came people like my parents, with their fine educations drawn from flinty little towns with gossipy cafés, manses, stout stone schools and fish suppers. Many of them did well in the professions and business. But on those nights when the whisky was low in the decanter, they would think of home, yearning for its familiar sounds and big hills, convincing themselves that it had been always been better than England.

So, when Scotland played England at rugby or football, they knew where their loyalties lay. For me it was different. I only saw Scotland as a tourist, though there was a feeling of deep affection held somewhere in the folk memory.

But I knew that England was my real home and I had developed a new kind of patriotism rooted in this country's humour, which I have always loved, from PG Wodehouse to Absolutely Fabulous by way of Evelyn Waugh, Tony Hancock, the Likely Lads, Peter Cook, Dad's Army and Fawlty Towers.

For this and other reasons I was delighted when this land, which has given the world so much, beat Australia. But could we arrange a transfer – Jonny Wilkinson for Bonnie Prince Charlie?

⌒

Christmas passed

We nosed from the house like moles, dragging tummies warmly fleshed by nuts, puddings and cakes, stuffing and the sleek vegetables laid beneath the trussed legs of a generous fowl, still plump on the table.

And then we sank our necks into thick woollen collars, shuddered, and blinked again against the cold of the outside world.

It was Saturday morning and, standing on the doorstep with my son, I could sense that Christmas was over, at least as a festival of peace and fellowship arising from a period of contemplation and celebration.

The Wise Men's gifts shone brightly in the cribs and my tipsy, creeping toes still felt the stairs stepped by Father Christmas in the hush of night. But the cash rolls were rolling once more, as though suddenly freed from their brief rest by a whoosh from a laxative of atomic force.

So, with shoulders squared, elbows primed and buttocks swinging, we lowered our heads and hoofed the ground like crazed bulls. The sales were here and we were thundering into the shops, with the muscle, sweat and puff of England's all-conquering rugby team. Perhaps, if coach Clive Woodward thinks they need sharpening up, he should consider training sessions in a shopping centre during this mayhem called the sales.

In such arenas, my slender wife's natural grace is a tremendous advantage. To the seasoned observer, she is the fly-half of the shopping queues. From the ruck you pluck a bargain and toss it over the

Life, love and washing up

heads of other customers to her cunning position, lurking on the fringes; from whence she sprints down the polished boards, feinting, swerving and demonstrating the occasional hands-off, leaving her rivals sprawling and gasping in her wake, until she touches down at the check-out counter.

This is madness. The strange thing is that we all know it and shake our heads in disbelief. Yet most of us do it anyway. From Christmas Eve, vulgar, strident, insistent TV advertisements had been tempting us to spend even more money at these sales.

Outside the store, in which we had begun some 'serious shopping', was the spot where Santa Claus had sat. His throne was empty and his sack crumpled, but the great, fawn-eyed animals of the woods stood there still, mute and unsmiling now, because their power had been killed by the flick of a switch after business on Christmas Eve.

Fleetingly, the thought that Santa and Satan are formed from the same letters slipped into my soul like sour milk, but the mood went quickly. It had been a splendid Christmas.

I spent most of it lying prone as my stomach spread across the lounge floor.

"Ahaa," you say in that inimitable manner. "Has he been at the decanters again, like a camel sucking on an oasis?"

"Not so," I reply. "I have been the very model of temperance. The Sally Army will be sending round a recruitment sergeant before long."

No, the trouble was that most of my seven-year-old son's presents were best played when your eyes were skimming the carpet's pile. For example, there was a magnet football game named after Michael Owen, the England striker, who will have zoomed up the national earnings' list as a result of this seasonal initiative.

I have a hazy recollection of an advertisement for this game, in which the players pinged the ball around the pitch with Beckham-style passes and bursts of acceleration which would leave a cheetah standing, encouraged by roars and chants from a huge crowd.

Well, in common with so much in today's world, this is true in part. For example, it would be unjust to suggest that any of the players had the 'dribbling skills of a lamp-post', a compliment I once heard paid to a distinguished England international by one of his admirers at Goodison Park. This 'supporter' advised us at another match of how he had been witness to another phenomenon on the football field.

"I have seen milk turning faster than that lad," he bellowed, despairingly, into winter's grip, as darkness fell all around us.

Anyway, in this game you have 11 players a side, like real football. Each is fitted with a spring for 'kicking' the ball and a magnet at his feet to attract passes. A quick tap on the head of the man in possession of the ball should, if properly aimed, send it to another player in the same team.

But, as any football manager will tell you, moves perfected on the practice pitch don't always come off in the heat of battle on Saturday afternoons. Our boy immediately grasped the finer points of the game, leaving me floundering on the grass. His men swung the ball around the field like Brazilians while glaciers could have blistered past my best efforts.

"Foul," he cried as I upended one of his temperamental, fancy-Dan stars in the penalty area.

And from the kitchen came the unmistakeable tones of our one fan. "Turkey, curried turkey, come and get it," called my wife at half-time.

Daddy long-legs and the new chair

"Tut, tut, tut. What shall we do with you? These legs are really far too long for your body," said my wife.

Then she attached a tape measure to the dimpled curve of my left buttock, which, in the warm haze of one memorable afternoon on the municipal tennis court, excited a wolf whistle from an elderly Girl Guide slumped in a bath-chair and no longer in complete control of her salivary glands.

From there, the tape was stretched to the steam gently curling from feet held in the grip of indestructible Terylene/mix socks, which had been presented to me in the Christmas of 1969, when dear Aunty Gwladys acquired of a job-lot of bankrupt clothing stock from a shadowy source, whose name she would whisper inaudibly while tapping her lesser-warted nostril.

"Yes, as I feared, you will never fit in the chair," my wife added. "We'll have to find another one for you."

"The chair!" I cried. A terrible picture filled my mind. I could almost feel the leather clasps being secured to my wrists, ankles and neck, so that I would sit securely in what I am told is called 'Old Sparky' in the alternative furnishing trade.

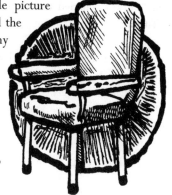

There was my wife controlling the current from the other side of a glass screen. "You will take me to Bloomingdale's department store in Manhattan," she said, with her delicately-jewelled fingers resting on a handle over an ominous series of voltage numbers.

"I will do no such thing," I replied with a defiant croak in my voice.

"Well, let's see if this helps change your mind," she said, suddenly pressing the handle down an inch, so that I jerked, convulsed and smouldered on the other side of the glass.

"That should do it."

In fact, the truth was a great deal worse than that. We are going to have a conservatory added to the back of the house and when you have a new conservatory you must have a new tea-service, a new TV, new sympathetic perfumes, new rugs and furniture to go in it, all according to the immutable laws of female logic.

Not only do you need new furniture, but you need new clothes, new blusher, new slippers, new lipsticks and new nail varnish to wear so that you complement your new surroundings. And, of course, there is no point in having a nice new cornflower couch if a shocking-pink old man is going to sit on it.

Before I continue on this theme, I should tell you that I have been sent back to the shop to exchange a consignment of lavatory rolls because the paper did not blend with the other colours in the bathroom, though in my opinion lime green goes with almost everything.

"What if we had visitors?" said my wife. "You couldn't expect a sensitive person to feel happy sitting on our loo facing paper of that shade."

Anyway, I was taken down to the warehouse to be fitted for the chair, which I must admit is rather well fashioned from wicker and equipped with a generously padded cushion.

"You see, I had hoped you'd squeeze into it because it has a nice matching couch and table," said my wife. "What a pity your legs are so long. Still, we can't really shorten you."

"Not on the NHS," I agreed.

Since the idea of the conservatory came up, our living-room has been taken over by brochures and diagrams, protractors and rulers.

Life, love and washing up

You would think that a kind of British rival to the Taj Mahal is going to sprout in the garden, where our rabbit lives. But I do have to admit that it does look good on the pictures, designed in an Edwardian style.

On the sadder side, it will bring to an end the games of football and cricket which I played with my seven-year-old son on the lawn. But maybe we are growing out of that sort of thing. The lawn, over which he once toddled, falling and crawling and giggling, is really very small. But there is a difference between the measurements of the memory and the true dimensions of life.

One of his friends has asked him to 'stay over', as the expression has it. This is another stage in a child's development. The boy takes another step into adult life and we wave from the window, breath clouding the glass. He waves back, all grown-up and cool. This is his first night away from home. The place is so empty without him. You can hear a cup clink on its saucer and the tinkle of the teaspoon.

Soon will come the day when he will pass through that door a man. But you don't think of such things, yet. There are years of boyhood to enjoy before that.

And our football field, beneath the quarried walls of sandstone, is a place where memories are held and, if you close your eyes, you can see the smile as it was and will always be.

Meanwhile, we have the conservatory to look forward to and in time it will mature into our memories.

Everything that is new grows old. But soon I will hear the sounds of young voices in our conservatory, this place of the future, where you can store the past, and that is good.

"You will look fine in the chair," says my wife.

⌣

The food of love

I was sucking contentedly on a humbug when the chilblain on the fourth toe of my left foot swelled into an itch of such irresistible potency that it would have excited a scratch from a granite Buddha.

Ministering to it, however, afforded me a brief break from contemplating the pleasures of the weekend ahead, such as humping rupture-weight furniture from one room to another at the whim of my wife.

No sooner was my sock removed for the scratching to begin than the man reading the TV news said that the next item could distress viewers of a sensitive disposition.

This is always the cue for turning up the volume and shuffling the chair nearer the screen. I waited for the blinking of a second and then a replete figure filled the screen.

This, we were told, was Armin Meiwes, a German who had been sentenced to eight years in prison for eating his friend, Bern Brandes.

I recoiled for a moment at the quaint use of the word 'friend', but quickly realised that one should make allowances for the customs of different countries, especially in these politically correct times when we are all part of a greater Europe.

"Eating people is wrong!" cried my wife, who is a vegetarian, after several minutes of thought at her desk, where she had been preparing my Saturday schedule.

"With you on that one, dear," I said.

"I suppose it wouldn't have been quite as bad if he had been really hungry like those poor chaps who get lost at sea for months and months and then finally draw straws to decide who should be lunch," she said. "But that man wasn't even peckish."

"By quirk of fate it was usually the cabin boy who was given the short straw as I recall from those old adventure yarns," I said, before inhaling a minty vapour from the striped humbug to clear my head.

"It seems that the two chaps met on a chat line on the internet," I continued. "Although it's not really my cup of tea, I understand that people with mutual interests can be introduced to one another electronically. For example, a toad-fancier in Bhutan could meet a like-minded spinster in Cleethorpes; or, if you suddenly found yourself short of a player of two for a rubber of bridge, one of these chat lines could be the answer. Britain's spoon bands would be in a parlous state without them.

"But Meiwes and Brandes were on a chat line where cannibals and would-be cannibals could compare notes and swap telephone numbers before taking their first faltering steps towards friendship. Taking all this into account, the judge found Meiwes guilty of manslaughter rather than murder because he accepted that Brandes wanted to be eaten in the ultimate gesture of 'bonding'."

By then the newsreader was advancing towards the weekend weather and my wife was staring from the window at the puddle spreading where our conservatory is to be built.

"Free societies may allow people to promote almost anything, however depraved, but I found the whole item rather chilling and very strange," she said.

Indeed, it was strange. Of course, if we are being truthful, there is a certain fascination in the discovery of a monster in human form, as long as he poses no threat to us. It is the horror film made flesh. The freak paraded as a vulgar entertainment, as he has been since the dawn of our being.

That is why this Meiwes was given such prominence in the newspapers and on the TV stations – with their warnings that the news could distress viewers.

More seriously, the occasional emergence of a fiend, who looks perfectly normal as he strides the pavement and chews his gum, reminds us that, despite the efforts of the powerful to create a uniform and obedient society, the human capacity for creating extraordinary people is undiminished. For Miewes is a human, who, for reasons beyond worldly grasp, has been driven by desires so disgusting that they escape our understanding. But we can be grateful that the vast majority of people on the far wings of life have been forces for the good, many surviving the discouragement of their elders and the mockery of the mob. Maybe, the creation of the occasional monster is the counter-balance to that. Who knows?

When I was little, the boys' comics almost invariably featured a Christian missionary simmering in a cooking pot while the tribe danced around the fire. Such images are no longer politically correct.

But in moments of high passion, I am told, lovers of a certain persuasion like to nip each other on the ear lobes and other parts of the anatomy. The big toe is sometimes mentioned in this connection.

The language of sex and love, too, is full of references to eating – what a dish, delicious figure, he's a gorgeous hunk, her skin's like honey, my boy lollipop. Even "sausage" can be used as a term of affection.

Anyway, as the news finished, I turned to my wife. "Would you care for a humbug, sweetheart?"

᠆᠆

Life, love and washing up

Gender benders

"They must have been wearing false beards," declared my wife, who, for a silent period of some 20 minutes, had been studying an article in the morning paper, while nibbling the fringes of a wafer biscuit to aid her concentration.

"To whom are you referring?" I asked, briefly raising my sweat-drenched head from the kitchen floor, where the remnants of a treacle toffee, dropped from my mouth when I was reading the phone bill, was successfully defying the energetic application of the scrubbing brush.

"The Three Wise Men," replied my wife.

"Good Lord," I said. "I'm sure that such manly chaps would have been able to grow their own beards. Why, the hair on their chests alone should have been enough to stuff a goodly mattress. By the way, I have often thought of plucking the hair from my own chest to insert in a locket for our wedding anniversary."

"No, you are missing the point, as usual," she scolded. "It says here that the Synod of the Church of England has decided that the Wise Men might have been women. Important people like that must know what they are talking about. Now, I suppose we'll have to change the words of the carol."

My wife tossed back her head and began to stretch her lips into a chorister's oval. As if by telepathy, our rabbit Jasper bounded across the garden and leapt into his hutch, muffing his ears. Seagulls, perched on the roof across the road, started flapping their wings for flight. The street sweeper gripped his chest.

"We three queens of Orient are . . ." boomed my wife.

"I wouldn't like to arrive on a stranger's doorstep with a couple of pals from the pub to sing that on Christmas Eve," I said. "Could cause something of a theological stir, especially when you consider how the word queen is popularly understood."

"But," continued my wife, "in all the photographs I have seen, Gaspar, Melchior and Balthasar have been shown standing around the baby Jesus, bearded."

"Photographs!" I responded. "A wee bit early for that. I think you will find that our own noble inventor William Fox Talbot didn't introduce the camera until about 1,800 years after the Nativity."

"Don't show off," warned my wife. "You know very well that I mean photographs of paintings by the great masters."

"Great mistresses," I corrected with an unexpected spurt of political correctness.

"The point is that women can't grow beards," said my wife.

"Hold on there," I said. "You don't remember Aunty Gwladys in her prime. You could have struck a match on her stubble. Talk about five o' clock shadow. Her chin was more like a total eclipse of the sun."

Anyway, it seems that in short prayers called collects, the dear old C of E is to call the Wise Men Magi, a word taken from the ancient Persian and used to describe priests, astrologers and magicians of either sex.

But should we stop at this? Surely the initiative by the Synod gives woman the opportunity to change the sex of many of the celebrated figures in history.

For example, my wife has long suspected that Napoleon was a woman since reading of how he suffered terribly from the cold, growing massive chilblains, during the retreat from Moscow, finally leaving the rest of his troops, so he could go home and enjoy an early bath in Paris.

"Women are more susceptible to the cold," she explained.

"Not really conclusive evidence, is it?" I told her. "Next you'll be

Life, love and washing up

suggesting that old Napoleon said, 'not tonight Joseph', on the eve of a big battle."

However, the sisterhood should be aware that two can play at this game. My own ambition is to prove that Hitler was a woman. After all he only had a little moustache, not one of those Old Testament beards in which you could cultivate spuds. Yes, he was good at goose-stepping and holding his right arm erect, foaming at the mouth and invading countries, but you don't hear much about Hitler bedding dazzling Aryan blondes.

Once it is established that Hitler was a woman, possibly a Girl Guide mistress, we'll have to reappraise our traditional thinking on gender. Men will attend crochet sessions while their women-folk head for the Duchess of Wellington pub to participate in the yard-of-ale contest or a spot of arm-wrestling.

In writing this, I am beginning to wonder whether my thinking has already been overtaken by events, with women running the show wherever you look. But I must admit to looking forward to the day when the gals wolf whistle and wink as I walk by.

Meanwhile, I have invented a game in which you can choose the sex of a famous or infamous figure from history. Vlad the Impaler, who enjoyed nothing better than listening to the squeals of the hapless souls slipping ever so slowly down the pole was obviously a woman.

Boudicea, brave patriot, who challenged the might of Rome, was surely a man, though others may wish to claim him as their 'queen'. It's very confusing.

〜

Fashion advice
from beyond the grave

We speak of these things called ghosts and they appear in the popular imagination as veiled figures in cold rooms who float, friendless, through eternity; stopping only to swap the ornaments on your mantel for a bit of 'divilment', as my half-Irish granny with the sacred prayer book would have said in the days long gone, when her refined nose enjoyed sniffing the scented powder on chunks of Turkish delight.

But to me these ghosts are just memories, which become vivid again as you concentrate very hard, alone, in the silence of night. In this way, you can almost resurrect people, certainly drawing them again into the light of your thoughts.

It is a year since my mother died and I often picture her, not in a mawkish spirit, but seeing again the smile of her humour. It was not a humour for guffaws and vulgarity or stock jokes with their lavatorial punctuation and weary punch lines, favoured by bores at pubs or tedious business meetings, at which promotions are given to those who laugh loudest and longest at the chairman's stories.

If someone sidles up to you and says, "Have you heard the one about . . .?", the only answer is "YES", before another word can escape his lips.

But my mother liked the quiet observation of human absurdity, particularly the failures of those who seek to succeed, desperately. So I have given her much cause for amusement down the years, from the egg-and-spoon race to my attempts to sing like Elvis.

As you grow older, however, it becomes increasingly difficult to take anything seriously.

For example, the International Olympic Committee is to consider whether transexuals should be allowed to compete in the Games without recourse to that surgery which, I am advised, can turn men into women and, even more remarkably, women into men. It's about 'human rights' and 'equal opportunities'.

All a chap would have to do is live like a woman for two years – or vice versa. On first examination, the idea is not without a certain charm. I could stand a few months of being given breakfast in bed, chocolates, jewels, a storm-proof conservatory and a kiss on the tip of the nose every morning, if it led to my selection for the ladies' ping-pong team.

And the news has given a terrific fillip to 'Hairy' Herbert, the blacksmith, who despite his passion for lager and gammon steaks soaked in more fat than a sumo wrestler's thighs, has long yearned to enter the world of figure skating in his skirt of lilac frills.

Of course, it won't all be one-way traffic. You might think that simpering, full-lipped Daphne in the customer complaints' department is the very essence of feminine beauty, but have you seen her tossing a caber?

My mother would have seen the comic possibilities of such developments in a world where the crazy is routine and good sense is as rare as a hair on Bobby Charlton's head.

Anyway, she came to my mind last week when I left the house for work wearing a baseball cap fashioned in a singularly unpleasant shade of green with a fawn peak stretching into the distance like a shop awning.

"Och, David, you are not really going out in that, are you? They'll take you away in a van," she would have said in her soft Glaswegian accent. "When you are wearing a hat, it is important to consider the feelings of others, whose sensibilities may be less robust than your own."

With these thoughts in mind, I removed the hat on the train, so as not to offend the man sitting opposite. The train jerked into motion and I laid the hideous green cap by my bag on the seat and closed my eyes for a few minutes rest.

We shuddered to a halt at the station and I grabbed the bag and headed for the door to the platform. But where was the hat? Had I suffered a lapse of memory or had some unseen hand taken it away to a charity shop on the other side?

It must have been the first of these possibilities, as my mother would not have been seen dead carrying a hat like that.

For the price of a pint

Gazing forlornly in the shaving mirror the other night, I was reminded of an article which I had read a day or two earlier saying that experts at the Louvre Gallery in Paris were considering methods of protecting the Mona Lisa against the ravages of time.

Of course, Leonardo da Vinci's enigmatic smiler is almost 450 years older than me, but the greying of hair, the rotting of teeth and a sagging of the jowls all show that I am closing the gap pretty fast.

"The only thing new on me is the pimple trying to break through the gap in my moustache," I muttered to myself, while in the next door room my wife was sprinting up and down the floor in pursuit of a wood louse, from whom she she was hoping to beat the leaving daylights with her lacrosse stick.

In the lurid language of today, she seemed to be suggesting that the poor little fella had been born outside wedlock. "Come here and face me, you b . . . d."

Anyway, give it another 10 years or so and the smart money would be laid on me looking a great deal older than Ms Lisa. But you have to agree that writing for a crust is a rather tougher business than posing before a renaissance master with a silly grin on your face.

That night at the mirror, I had been preparing for one of those rare events, a visit to the pub. Our eight-year-old son was staying the night at the home of a friend, so there was an opportunity to step out. We chose a black and white pub with beams and horse brasses, where even a beer-belch carries a hint of gentility.

"That will be £7.35," said the barmaid. But to whom was she addressing that demand, I wondered, looking around the packed room. Had someone ordered a bottle of Chateau Mouton Rothschild?

Her eyes were clinging to me like a pair of barnacles on a rusting hulk. "I think that must be for someone else," I said. "I only ordered two large glasses of red wine and a packet of ready-salted crisps."

"Yes that's right. It's seven pounds and thirty five pence," she said, emphasising each word, as if to a child. Scraping the mildew from my wallet, I plucked out a £10 note. Then, as she went to fetch the change from the till, I searched among the bus-tickets, peanuts, used blister-pads and coins in my back pocket for a suitable tip.

Before I could retrieve a 10p, she had gone to serve the other customers, leaving my change on the counter. Oh, what a busy world we live in!

"Now, in the old days," I said to my wife, as we sat at a table in a far corner of the room. At that very moment, for reasons that I don't fully understand, she released a groan which was quite audible.

But I ploughed on regardless, "you could have almost bought a car with the money that this lot cost".

This, in fact, was true. A friend of mine had bought a car for £10 in 1965, though I have never owned one myself, being temperamentally unsuited to the wheel.

That was the era when a stranger to these islands would have wondered if our cars were built with human legs jutting out of the front. Every Saturday and Sunday mornings, down the avenues and streets of any town, you could see young men with oil rags and spanners lying under their cars tinkering with the engines. A car was a hobby then. Now it's an extension of life itself.

The car bought by my friend was a side-valve Morris Minor, which he drove for at least two years.

An old colleague, however, was less fortunate when, in the back of a car showroom, he spotted an ancient three-wheeler dripping its parts. A tag hanging from the remnants of its bonnet was marked 'fourpence (or nearest offer)'.

By three-wheeler, I mean a motorised tricycle, rather than a four-wheeler deficient at one corner. This was not, it has to be admitted, a canny purchase. However, after some tough haggling, he persuaded the ruddy-faced proprietor in the pork-pie hat to accept a penny less than what he had called "the recommended price".

"Ah, God bless you for your cheek, sir. I admire a chap who drives a hard bargain," said the man, stifling a laugh, as he rubbed the stubble on his chin with the back of the hand that he used for signing guarantees.

Indeed, the bargain was the only thing driven by my poor colleague after he paid for the wreck to be carted to his house.

The cost of going out and the way it compares to other prices is one of the important measures in life. When I was a cub reporter, the old men would tell me of how they set out with some ludicrously small sum like three shillings (15p). With this, they would buy a packet of Woodbines, a few pints, a seat at the music hall, fish and chips, and still have enough left for the bus fare home.

But as the drinks go down and the evening slips into a convivial flush, it becomes easier and easier to pay for the drinks.

"And would you care for a wee one yourself," you say to the barmaid, as an old melody brushes your memory.

Life, love and washing up

Damned statistics

The other day I lowered myself, ever so gingerly, into the sofa's old velvet cushion, which sinks slowly, with the sympathy of experience, to the requirements of my weary limbs.

Once comfortable, I had intended reading a lengthy survey which said . . .

But at this point I should pause to ask a question. Why are there so many surveys, providing such a glut of useless information? Every morning, you can depend on a fresh crop rising like mushrooms in horse manure, daisies on a vicarage lawn, or pimples on a new shaver's chin.

Many of these surveys deal with social and consumer trends and the regional variations in our health.

So we never know what thrills the next headline will hold: ingrowing toenails crisis in Cleethorpes; Bootle, the doughnut capital of western Europe; Fazakerley folk use more strips of toilet paper per head than anywhere else in Britain (are they applying the strips to the wrong place or is it those legendary Friday night vindaloo sprees?).

Some years ago, a real survey in Wirral concluded, with an almost Biblical insight, that people from the affluent suburbs tend to be healthier and to live longer than those in the poor, dockland areas. This, however, was a "feel good" report designed to make everyone happy and bouncy, so the researchers were presented with the problem of spreading their message of joy all around. It was solved with considerable ingenuity.

They discovered an area spreading along the waterfront of Birkenhead, where the incidence of skin cancer was the lowest in the UK because nobody could afford foreign holidays. This was something to whoop-up the spirits of the down-trodden, as they watched the rain trickle, greyly, down their windows, overlooking the municipal tip.

At that level, spin-doctoring is indeed a dark art, worthy of a place in Downing Street, if not the White House.

Pollsters and researchers can be recognised by their splay feet, American smiles, a sheen of sweat, clipboards and mock deference, which mix together into the missionary zeal necessary to ask total strangers about their personal habits.

I was approached by one at the railway station. By what means, he wanted to know, had I arrived there. This was the sort of question you would reserve for the pointy-headed, purple chap with an ice cream cornet, leading a gaggle of day-trippers from Pluto.

What should my answer be — spacecraft, balloon, hydrofoil, pogo-stick?

"Tricycle," I replied. "You see, I have been cursed with a very poor sense of balance."

Bus, I suspect, was the answer they were hoping for, as it could then have been fed into the dull-witted computer, presently plodding out statistics on the use of public transport, to be filed into oblivion by some clerk suffering from despair, terminal dandruff and bad breath, who hopes that before the trumpet calls from above, one of his jokes will be printed inside a Christmas cracker.

But the survey I had intended reading, as I sank into the couch with a cup of tea steaming on the table at my side, was of more interest than most. It claimed that the average cost of bringing up a child from birth to university was £164,000, about £18,000 more than a typical house.

The research, carried out for Woolworths, was based on the experiences of 3,000 British mothers. In the first five years of the child's life, the parents had on average spent £8,000 in nursery charges. The fees for a part-time nanny to look after the child between the ages of five and 11 were put at £46,368, based on 20 hours with one evening's babysitting a week. In the teenage years, most of the money had gone on fashions, sports kits, electronic gadgets and pocket money. All this had been leading towards the university/college years, between 19 and 21. Then, the young person cost his parents £20,000 in fees and living expenses and £10,000 for food, clothes and general expenses.

Of course, we spend our money in different ways. For example, I have never called on the services of a nanny, yet this survey gives us a glimpse of a selfish, modern Britain, in which people of a certain stamp use unpleasant, but meaningless, expressions such as "quality time". By this they mean time devoted entirely to themselves.

You can't measure all things by money. In the emotional sense, children are in a constant state of repaying the parents. Their successes and their sorrows become part of you. In my eight-year-old son, I can see a little bit of me continuing in the world. God help everyone else. God help him, even more than that.

On Saturday mornings, down on the field, with a football at our feet, beneath the quarried walls, where the grass is damp and nature is true, you don't think of money at all because everything has been given.

And those silly surveys are written so that people will know what to buy in their 'quality time'.

↬

Intelligent foreplay

A long time ago, when romance was still green and eager in my hopes, I was drinking peasant wine on a table outside a white-washed stone cafe in the ancient Roman city of Dubrovnik. There, the old men with black suits and loose teeth played chess, moving their veined, sun-leathered hands over the boards, while admiring the generous swing on the hips of passing women.

"Arrrgghh," they sighed, from deep inside their memories.

With me was my friend Brian, called The Horse because he had big front teeth for chomping apples. I suppose the anxious parents of the time had seen us as a pair of nice, if feckless, lads, a little too fond of the drink and not sufficiently dedicated to the real world of commerce and careers.

Anyway, we had pitched our tents with the hippies in a camp on a hill overlooking this port of oil and dust and flies by the Adriatic Sea, before walking to the cafe.

Suddenly, there was a rap on the corrugated iron roof followed by another and another. We ducked inside the building to be away from the rain now falling from a sky the colour of Welsh slate, fractured here and there by shards of lightning.

Soon the little road outside was a stream and, as we took our new seats, the electricity failed. This then was part of Communist Yugoslavia and nobody was very surprised by failures, whatever the apparatchiks might have said.

The waiters lit candles on each table.

And we settled on our chairs, preparing for a long session on the red wine. After a few minutes we became aware that two sisters were standing over us, both staring from eyes of Hollywood blue.

"We were wondering if you boys would permit us to join you?" asked the older of the two sisters.

We had seen them first that morning, emerging in swimming costumes from the tent alongside ours – honey blondes.

"We're from Pickens, South Carolina," said the lead sister, brushing a few grains of sand from a knee, surely sculpted in heaven. In her voice was the confidence of generations of privilege and pride, reaching back to a time when her ancestors' ears warmed to laments from the plantations.

There was a pause of seconds as Brian and I silently exchanged eloquent glances.

"We're from Birkenhead," he said, finally. Well, in my experience that had always been sufficient to end any promising romance.

But here they were sitting at our table. What should we talk about? I knew that Brian had once read in a magazine's agony column that women weren't really interested in men's bodies, kissing techniques or looks. Instead, they wanted someone who was clever with a keen sense of humour.

That was fine. I hadn't stopped laughing since I first saw myself in a full-length mirror.

And Brian fancied himself as a bit of a historian, having passed his history O level at the second attempt.

As I attempted to attract the attention of a waiter for more wine, Brian accidentally dropped his cigarette lighter, indicating with a jerk of his head that I should join him under the table to search for it.

"I think I shall give mine a potted history of the world," he whispered.

"Keep it potted," I advised.

After about a few minutes, the older sister, who was by me, said to the other one: "What's happening with you two?"

"Well, we're with the hunter/gatherers in the African savannah at the moment. I can't wait to hear what happens next. What about you?"

"Hmmm, my guy is leading me across the Alps with Hannibal's army and it seems that I'm ridin' on a mighty fine elephant," she said.

We all smiled at the absurdity of it and the sisters, who were charming in every way, seemed pleased to be with us, despite all the hulking Australian and American beach boys who had been rippling along the parade until it looked like a body-builders' convention.

Now I discover that we might have been right all along. After eight years of tests, Pfizer, maker of Viagra, the pill which has transformed the sex lives of flagging males, has concluded that an equivalent drug is unlikely to work for women.

Dr Mitra Boolel, leader of the company's sex research team, said: "The brain is the crucial sex organ in a woman."

Females, the report added, gain most sexual satisfaction from mental stimulation. It is with this in mind that I am preparing a series of quadratic equations to be completed by my wife before bedtime every night.

"Foreplay, what nonsense! Give me a crossword puzzle!" will become the cry of amorous housewives across the land.

In the past I have always assumed that a gentle, brushing kiss on my wife's lips, as she rests her her head on the pillow to close her turquoise eyes, will please her more than anything. In future, though, I will follow that up by asking her to name all the British home secretaries since the war, in the right order.

〜

A good man

He had broad shoulders of the sort that could swell any jacket of Donegal tweed and his hands, which stretched from sleeves padded in leather at the elbows, were big and veined and very strong and they could lift a hod of bricks and rest it on some place so surely that the dust would barely move.

But these same hands could rub the back of a cantankerous old dog's ears until the growls became sighs of pleasure and then he would gaze up with faith and affection, through the soft brown of his eyes.

And when the man looked at a house he could tell you in a few moments whether the beams were strong enough for a new generation or whether those creaking boards had been wormed by too many years.

Now he was encased in wood himself, lying in a polished box, under the timber-panelled ceiling in the aisle of a stone church, where they were playing a Highland lament on the pipes.

This was a good man who seemed to have been shaped and fleshed by his Creator to fit the dictionary definitions of 'strong'.

People shuffled into the church and took their places, looking around to see who else was there, in the way you do at a funeral, while the family sat at the front, holding their more precious and personal memories.

There was that slow, low hum of conversation you always get in church. People imagine that God likes you to whisper in his many houses. This may be right. I don't know. It's just a mood that cloaks everyone present.

But nobody could doubt on this day that they were all there to say their earthly farewells to a good man. There was special sadness, too, because just four days after he left us, his great grand-daughter was born.

And she was there at the front, tiny, wrapped in white and breathing gently in a cradle, to say goodbye before she had said hello.

Outside, the Belgian black ponies stood in their blinkered patience, waiting to pull the carriage once the man had been laid there. Then, to another place, whose style and furnishing and company we can only imagine in the dark and stormy nights of our lonely thoughts. The horses lifted one hoof and then the other, to keep each leg fresh for the journey, which would begin in a few minutes.

Inside, they were reading from *Death Is Nothing At All*, the poem written by Henry Scott Holland, former Canon of St Paul's Cathedral . . . " I have only slipped away into the next room, I am I, and you are you, whatever we were to each other that we are still . . ."

These words with their simple message of continuance bring so much comfort to people. I had known the man for all my remembered life, but never very well. He came round to see us every Christmas and each time, as he sat on the couch with a plate of mince pies, a slice of cake and a cup of sweet tea, he would remark on how fast our son was growing.

It was always a nice occasion. But I recalled the earlier days of this man, born as one of eight brothers and sisters into farming stock in Northern Ireland. He had worked on a farm himself, before joining the police force.

There had been times of high-thrills and near-terror when, as a little boy, I clung to his mighty frame on the pillion seat, as he rode his motorbike into town, with his wife sitting in the comparative luxury of the sidecar.

Life, love and washing up

And his wife, who had left him a widower 10 years earlier, was a real Irish colleen with her flowing dark hair and hazel eyes. Yes, they must have looked a handsome couple, when sprung by youth and hope, striding the streets, smiling, arm-in-arm.

But now both were gone and a voice, a lilting Irish tenor was singing to the *Londonderry Air*: "You raise me up so I can stand on mountains, you raise me up to walk on stormy seas, I am strong when I am on your shoulders, you raise me up to more than I can be . . ."

This is the song to draw tears from granite and most people there obliged, for a few seconds. But this was also a dignified occasion for the man, who loved learning and history and worried a little about the ways of the world.

"You look more beautiful each time I see you," he said to my wife at Christmas as they hugged at the door of our new house. We remembered then how his skill as a builder had helped us turn our first house into a home.

Sometimes I wondered if he saw a reflection of his own wife in her eyes. But you can never know about such things.

We were singing *Morning Has Broken* and the pall-bearers were waiting to carry the man away. With his own hands, he had built bungalows for his family, humping the stones and preparing the designs and smoothing the wet concrete. In fact, people thought that there was nothing he couldn't do. Now the time had come for his beloved daughter to lead the family, and she was bearing up well, as people say at funerals.

It was only at this service that I learned his full, noble name. William Charles Forrester Campbell, a good man.

Night-cap theologians

When I was a young man and tea was loose, the banks were tight, and ice cream came in the three main flavours of pink, white and brown, we sometimes adopted the pose of night-cap theologians to consider the idiosyncrasies of the various Christian sects.

Those were the days of foggy nights when the last bus home was always accelerating away from the stop at exactly the moment you arrived there, panting, with enough beer in your belly for it to ripple and gurgle like a hot-water bottle.

To catch this bus, you had to sprint and make a shut-your-eyes-and-pray leap for the platform at the back, before swinging on the passengers' chromium pole, where the conductor would mumble something about silly young fools, before demanding the number of pennies necessary to carry us home.

He would then crank out the tickets on the handle of the box which hung from his neck, examining its digits, twiddling knobs, shaking his head and sighing, in the style of a tourist with a complicated German camera.

We would head for the back seat on the upper deck to continue the discussion begun hours before in the pub. One of our group had a reputation for being worldly wise and when he spoke we listened.

On a particular night he decided to tell us a little about the doctrinal and social differences which could be found in three Christian churches – the Methodists, the Presbyterians and the Roman Catholics.

Sucking on a cigarette until it glowed like a blow torch, he stretched his legs and offered us the following observations from his many experiences of life.

The Presbyterians, he said, were against the devil's brew, intemperate language and stocking tops revealing thigh; but they were very much for stout shoes, sound business practice, Scottish victories over England, and nice floral displays.

The Methodists were against gambling, painted lips, red garters and ruthless capitalists; but they were for stirring hymns, fresh air, picnics and youth clubs.

The Catholics were quite happy about the drink, he said, from the priests down to the humblest kneelers. And they didn't mind a spot of fruit cake and bingo either, especially if it was to raise cash for a new church organ. However, they were vehemently opposed to sex outside marriage.

"But there is an active ecumenical movement," our friend said, "which could mean them all uniting in the future. What a rich mix that would make."

"It would result in all our pleasures being crushed," added one of us, who had enjoyed success with the bottle and the horses, without yet threatening the virtue of any young ladies, as far as we knew.

"Or," I replied, bleakly. "We could have a hymn-singing businessman in stout shoes sharing a bottle of elderberry wine with a voluptuous flower-arranger at a youth club picnic, watched by a bingo caller in a dog-collar."

At the end of such journeys we all hoped that a dare devil would ask us back for a night-cap, so that we could continue the discussion. And, more often than not, the whisky bottle would be uncorked and the conversations would roar through to midnight.

Missing from this analysis, as some of the more ecclesiastically-minded of you will have noted, was the dear old Church of England, which, at the time, was shifting from its traditional position of the Tory Party at prayer to its present role as the Liberal Party in a dither. But its general stance, then as now, seemed to be that pleasures were fine as long as you accepted them in a spirit of moderation.

Of course, as there were members of each of these denominations in our group, we recognised that our friend's analysis was really a load of baloney, though it made for entertaining conversation.

But this is the time of year when the big organisations, secular and religious, join the spiritual hope felt by us all in celebration of the coming Nativity.

The survival of our Christmas festival, not drastically changed since Victorian times, is one of the great modern miracles. Although it is attacked by the powers of commerce, the doubters and the mockers, this simple, but beautiful, story of a boy born to a virgin in a stable to save mankind, resists all hostile interference.

The genius of capitalism has been to promote Father Christmas almost to the status of God's representative in a crimson cloak, who can cross the snowless lands on a sleigh in one night to bring joy to every child.

When my little boy told me that he was starting to doubt the existence of Father Christmas, it nearly broke my heart. "But it isn't logical for him to go from England to India overnight," he said, with the sudden sagacity of the seven-year-old.

"But son, if you believe in him, he will be real for you," I said. "Always believe, as I do." I think then that he was convinced again. You see, after all these years, a night-cap theologian understands such things.

Everyone's a winner

Swimming has always been a problem for me. When crawling with my arms, I invariably forget to flip with my feet, thus progress is laboured.

Our boy, on the other hand, took to water like a frog, mastering the breast-stroke as if born in water. Having already gained a certificate for swimming a mile in the municipal pool, he has been awarded his bronze badge and his now heading for silver.

We watched with the pride of parents as he achieved his badge by swimming to a high standard in both the breast and back strokes. It was one of those hugging scenes of celebration, when a lump of pride lodges in your throat and tears shine your eyes. But then you wonder where it will lead.

Prizes come at a very high cost in terms of human tension and emotion. For months you think it is the only thing that matters in life. Your sleep is dampened by sweat, as your mind twists and arches towards that moment on the rostrum when some VIP will shake your hand and whisper the words of congratulation.

But then the emotion subsides and the laureate is left with the feeling that he must do something else to better his previous triumph and so it goes until you sense, deep within yourself, that the days of trophies have gone.

Like everyone else I felt sorrow and sympathy for Paula Radcliffe when she felt unable to complete the Marathon at the Olympic Games. The pursuit of prizes is cruel. For every success, there are hundreds of failures, just moments lost in time and crushed under the heels of the winners.

So there are sweet consolations in having an uncompetitive nature. You can feel the wet grass squelch beneath your feet as you run to fetch the cricket ball thumped into the yonder by your son.

And in the slow, warm mornings, you can watch the rise of the sun, knowing that it comes for everyone, not only those who run and jump and jostle for prizes and power.

⌐

Anorak pride

The man who collects fossilized eggs has brief conversations with his wife.

For it seems that the ardour, which once had bonded them in frolicsome pursuits and carefree bouts of ear-nibbling, wanes as the ancient ova gather in shoe-boxes under the rarely-troubled springs of their matrimonial bed, awaiting delivery to some learned society.

Perhaps you can see our man now in his woolly hat, hunkered under his pea-green anorak in some remote field, thumbing soil from the pitted shell of the egg delivered in another age by some hapless, web-footed squawker. The steam of anticipation is clouding the horn-rimmed spectacles secured by a strip of Elastoplast to the bridge of his long-dripping nose.

Suddenly his portable phone chirrups in the stillness. Birds flutter in the trees, alarmed worms retreat into the dark of their chilly tunnels. The man creaks from the mud to his gum-booted feet and scratches his bottom to the gentle purr of seasoned corduroy.

Cursing under his pickled breath, he begins rummaging among the bus tickets, spoons, handkerchiefs, pipes, pips, peel, dented tobacco tins, pippins, tools, spare socks, a folded note reminding him of his name, pills and trowels, seeking the offending phone in all of his 17 pockets.

Life, love and washing up

By choice he would not have the phone with him at all, but his wife insists that he should carry it everywhere because of his tendency to confuse where he is with where he should be.

When he has unearthed it, their conversation is curt. "Eight o' clock," he says to the twitterings mounting in speed and volume at the other end. "Yes, yes, yes, I will not forget it's Dolly's birthday. Goodbye."

Men are more inclined than women to follow those hobbies judged to be eccentric by the wider public, who prefer the television, work, texting messages, meetings, celebrity magazines and making the sign of quotation marks in the air with their index fingers when they think they have plucked up a particularly engaging word.

Of course, we are talking here of twitchers, train-spotters, moth-netters, bat-watchers, flat-earthers, model train and Dinky toy enthusiasts, quiz-team captains, marrow-growers, potion-brewers, philatelists, parsnip-wine drinkers, bell-ringers, unicyclists, ramblers, students of nature in general and chaps with stubbled chins building pedal-powered space rockets in their garden sheds.

Collectively such people are called "anoraks". This is an attempt by regular types to suggest that they are boring. "Cross to the other side of the road when you see a man in an anorak approaching you with his mouth agape," they say, sucking their cherry sticks among the bare-brick and varnished wood of a trendy bar, where emasculated jazz whispers through the speakers.

It is true that the anorak is a garment favoured by those on the fringes of society who enjoy talking to themselves for the want of better company; but, far from being dull, their wearers have had the self-confidence to escape the dictates of fashion and few things are more boring than that.

The danger is that the anorak should become the height of fashion and then the entertaining toad-fancier, with his riveting tales of natterjack courting rituals, would not be able to warn his pals about the dreaded advance of a public relations officer or a newly promoted advertising executive.

Women, generally being more sensible than men, are less enthusiastic about spending their weekends squelching through swamps, their heads wrapped in mosquito nets and their pockets stretched by emergency rolls of lavatory paper. Maybe that is why they do not take so easily to the anorak.

Of course, there are exceptions. We hear of great female explorers, mountaineers, marrow-cultivators, shoppers, flower-arrangers and sailors. From time to time, readers even enquire after my own dear Aunty Gwladys, the most revered wart-lancer in Birkenhead, who keeps her pet pterodactyl Joey in a cage in the parlour, where, for the past 40 years, she has been teaching him to say, "Who's a pretty boy?".

He remains steadfastly silent, save for the occasional oath, delivered under his breath as his angry, bloodshot eye follows Auntie Gwladys to the peg on which she hangs her purple anorak.

Anorak wearers are a welcome relief from those people who doubtless imagine that they are stylish and interesting when they appear in the pub dressed in track suits, their bellies a-wobble like a parade of jellies in an earthquake.

Well, the first goosepimples of winter are moaning on the wind these nights and in the mornings, before the sun has stretched over the roofline, there is a crackling of frost on the grass.

And hanging there in the cloakroom, waiting patiently, loose shouldered like a trusty friend, is my anorak, and I know that lurking in one of the pockets there is a vintage toffee.

A penchant for murder

It is strange and perhaps bemusing to the citizens of other countries, where parades of feather-hatted soldiers, exotic priests, polished boots and vivid icons are preferred, that the English genius for nostalgia should find its highest and most enduring celebration in murders.

Yes, the Americans may delight in their sentimental animated cartoons, gross food, rock 'n' roll, psycho-analysis, crazed evangelists, the god-almighty dollar, sun tan and smart bombs, but we offer the world our love of a good killing.

These killings can be divided into two broad types – the rural and the urban.

The first sort happen in country villages, still dreaming in the steam of tea-shops and dung under the sepia cloud which spread over them between the wars. Here, the flush-faced milkmaid, with full breasts for her brood to come, sits astride her three-legged stool, pulling on udders and sucking a straw, always hoping to persuade the slow-witted farmhand to remove his wellies and unhitch his braces for a spot of sport in the barn.

And then we come to the Victorian city; gin-breathed, teeming with shawlies, high-kicking chorus gals on the make, watches on chains, the toffs and the ruined, all lost in the fog that never lifts. We hear a shriek in the dark, the blast of the Peelers' whistles and a sudden scurrying of feet.

For Jack the Ripper, whoever he was, provided our people with a shadowy figure, bizarrely loved in his menace with a kind of immortality bestowed upon his character by anonymity.

In an essay written in 1946, George Orwell lamented the Decline of the English Murder, observing how the readers of Sunday papers enjoyed a poisoning or a skillfully executed killing, carried out by a figure of the utmost respectability who had been tempted away from Rotarian dinners and the tennis club accounts by a red-lipped floozy.

Orwell lamented the brutal and crude form of murder then coming into fashion.

But even this prophet of English manners and traits failed to anticipate our full genius for nostalgia.

Faced with gang warfare, doorway shootings, the almost unthinkable killing of children and the elderly, we have simply reverted to style by inventing murders of a more genteel nature, to be savoured as the butter soaks into the hot scones.

It is true that some of these were written in Orwell's time, some before, but they have been given a new charm on TV, which, for all its faults, remains very good at adapting a chilling murder for a new audience.

Last Saturday evening I was walking home with our seven-year-old son after Tranmere Rovers' victory against Chesterfield; crunching the leaves, both buttoned to the chin with hands deep in pockets. Dusk fell as we stepped, looking forward to easing away those instant woes and highs of football by watching *Miss Marple* with our mugs of cocoa and biscuits at hand.

The late Joan Hickson was wonderful as Jane Marple, the purse-lipped and tweedy flower-pruner of St Mary Mead. Every tilt of her bird-like head and every slight gesture is timed to perfection, while a deep understanding darkens the blue in the eyes of this sage of gossip, who has a mind as keen as a razor.

Agatha Christie's other great creation is Hercule Poirot, played in the TV adaptations of the Belgian detective's cases by David Suchet, who has enough charm to stir anyone's little grey cells.

The novels are in a sense puzzles, introducing a cast of stock characters – the vicar, the churlish housemaid, the moody poet or painter, the brash American businessman, the unscrupulous solicitor, the roué, the romeo, the vamp, the retired colonel, the heiress. They can all be switched around the chess board. The action is set in a country house, a seaside hotel, or a thatched village where the church bells peal for evensong.

Once on TV, the stories satisfy the yearning, planted in many of us from childhood, for a mythic past, far away from the realities of day-to-day life in the technological age.

Similar qualities add to the appeal of a whole host of TV detective stories including *Midsomer Murders*, *Morse*, *Wycliffe*, the *PD James Mysteries* and *Jonathan Creek*.

Certainly there are TV murder dramas which would appear to be more "relevant" to our times, most notably *Cracker*, *A Touch of Frost* and *Prime Suspect*. To some extent, however, all these deflect attention from the gore by concentrating attention on the main characters, played by Robbie Coltrane, David Jason and Helen Mirren.

Each is attached to a large, soulless group and is regarded by his/her peers as a misfit because of sex, age, attitude, a wrecked private life or a generous helping of insubordination.

So the setting is modern, but the mood reaches back to the past because, as a nation, we have always admired eccentric individuals and dislike big organisations.

Elementary, dear reader.

﹏

On the touchline

If you lack the organisational talent to round-up a gaggle of nuns for vespers, you can only marvel at the scene.

It emerges when the heavy, dripping mists of young winter rise like a silent curtain to reveal a cast of many colours and stripes parading on the squelching, glooping mud that some poet of the streets once described as 'the theatre of dreams'.

This is the first miracle of the weekend.

Thousands of children, some little more than eye-high to a door-knob and others, lanky and voiced as sweetly as a rusty tomb-lid, whiskers prodding out of their pimples, gather on hundreds of pitches to play football for teams, which are methodically listed into a network of leagues and divisions, representing talent, age and locality.

Every match is recorded, the results and the scorers noted, the points awarded in the ceaseless pursuit of medals and trophies. And the teams move up and down the tables, like blood pressure measured in triumph and despair.

Most of the players are boys, but an increasing number of girls can be spotted in the ranks, pigtailed or with their hair bound back in flowing ribbons. Otherwise, the sexes are indistinguishable in their boots, shin-pads, socks, shorts, shirts and training tops, as they are ushered to the spaces between the pitches for some pre-match exercises and instruction from the manager and his assistants.

On the municipal fields, where my son plays for the under-nines of an old and proud club, they speak of a girl called Charlotte, whose dribbling and combative tackling is already legendary, though she is still some years short of her first crush on a pop star.

"Will she be playing today?" they ask.

As the big moment draws near, the players are called into huddles, arms around each other and heads down, expressions of grim determination, as they listen to the final tactical tips from their manager, usually a former amateur player held in respect by his contemporaries.

"Now watch that number seven, he's like a whippet. Take no nonsense from the big striker or he'll be all over you. Keep the ball moving. Hold your concentration. Play to the whistle. Remember to keep your positions and play for each other and play fair. We don't want any prima donnas out there. Now do your best. Go to it."

The children are driven to the fields by their parents who arrive at about 8.30am. Mothers are almost as much in evidence as the fathers. For there is keen parental competition down the touchline. Everyone wants his son or daughter to shine. After all, it is only natural to want your own to do well.

But the word 'son' is used as a general address of endearment for a player on your side. Mate or pal are alternatives, delivered with affection or frustration, depending on the tone of voice. The boy who scores is everyone's son for a few moments of celebration, before he is urged to return to the fray, cool of head and sound of limb.

"I knew that lad would turn out good the first time I saw him. He's got footballer stamped through him like a stick of rock, just like his brother," declares a veteran of the parks, stroking his nose in a highly sagacious manner.

The supporters of the respective teams straddle down the touchline on opposite sides of the pitch, bellowing their encouragement or their disappointment or their opinions about the decisions of the referee, in a variety of guttural tones.

So much seems to be at stake here. "But it's only a game," they say, shaking their heads when the opposition's tricky playmaker sets up a goal.

You know, though, that it's more than a game to them, far more. It may not be more important than life or death, as the late Bill Shankly once suggested, apparently in all seriousness, when discussing his philosophy as the manager of Liverpool. But it would take more than the invasion of the shopping centre by green men from Mars to persuade them to leave these fields – unless, of course, the strangers had come down looking for a game.

"Don't think I'm being cheeky, pal, but what are we going to do about the away fixture?"

Back on Earth, the matches are under way. The players shake hands, wearing shirts decorated with the names of sponsors – maybe a firm in double-glazing, plumbing or house construction.

At half-time, the sweating players suck juice from plastic bottles shaped like space-ships and the manager tells them what they are doing right or wrong.

Word hums among the crowd that a scout is here from one of the big Premiership clubs. Well now, this is the theatre of dreams and hopes and prayers for the players and parents. But as the idea takes grip, the club secretary comes round shaking a bag for your match subscription. Frosted air billows from her mouth.

Above all else, these Saturday mornings are a triumph of organisation by the unsung men and women behind the scenes.

～

Fishing for compliments

My father once knew a man who sold worms to supplement the income he made from trading in maggots and the other mysterious enterprises which enabled him to spend hours of his days and most of his nights perched on a stool at the bar of the little pub, where his enormous hands, hardened on the handle of his digging fork, clasped a dimpled pint pot.

To be sure, this was not steady work in the same way as accountancy, busking or managing the marketing department of a toffee empire. But by clipping hedges, clearing ditches and removing the weeds from a man-made lake high in the hills of North Wales, he appeared to be a figure of substance – always dressed in a cap with a sweat-stained leather rim, an ancient tweed jacket and baggy brown corduroy trousers tucked into wellies, which accommodated feet so long that you wondered if they had been fitted with an extension.

In the days before sophisticated TV advertising, it was widely known that he dealt in the worms and maggots favoured by fishermen wishing to try their luck in the numerous streams which gargled down the purple-heathered mountains in ceaseless melody.

These squirming creatures were, of course, the bait and he kept them in large containers from which they would be scooped into smaller tins fitted with ventilated tops. Thus, the bait was kept fresh and succulent for the trout – or the trouts, as some people said.

Those were the days when large numbers of

people gathered to worship, solemnly and in their Sunday best, at the thousands of biscuit brown chapels which served all the villages of North Wales. Now most of them have been converted into offices or houses, but I wonder occasionally whether the bait man would have knelt in one of these places to pray to his God for a goodly supply of pink worms.

Anyway, there was an evening, sultry and sweating with flies agitating around the cowpats, when I was a little boy and my father was in his fifties. We walked to adjacent fields watered by the same stream and I carried my first fishing rod, bought earlier that day in Woolworths.

Sitting on the bank, I pressed the hook through the saddle of a suitably tempting worm and dangled into a deep pool, a few feet away from the main rush of the fast water.

In the contest between man and fish, we have the bigger brains and are stronger on book-learning, but they have the sharper instincts. So, I can only conclude that the next happening was what is known in the game as 'beginner's luck'.

Suddenly, there was a twitch on the line and I pulled in a trout, which, though bigger than a sardine, would have been wary of bullying pilchards.

"Daddy, daddy, I have caught a fish," I bellowed, rushing up the rise to his field, with my prey still struggling on the hook. "Indeed, you have," said my father, adjusting his spectacles, "and now all the fish in all the streams and all the rivers and all the seas in the world know of your triumph."

He was a man for quiet celebration.

"A tasty morsel," said my mother, as she sizzled the poor wee fella in a pat of butter. With deft strokes of my knife, I removed his flesh from the bone. On such occasions, it is customary to say that you have never eaten a better fish. But that is the sentiment of romance. I was not then, and have never been since, a great admirer of fishy flavours, though I admit there is a certain delicacy in the mountain trout.

At weddings and funerals, I shy away from the salmon sliced on a plate and decorated, for those of sensitive appreciation, with green sprigs.

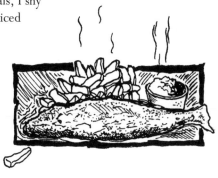

On a coarser note, I was alarmed recently to observe a waitress in a cafe dolloping plates with a bubble-gum-pink substance which had been scooped liked mashed potato from a vat. It was described as tuna and sold very well.

However, in line with most of my generation, I do have a liking for cod, as served in a chip shop. It's the batter. Ideally, the fish should be crisp at both ends, with the batter thinning, as it spreads towards the swollen middle, where the soft, white flesh awaits your bite. A light sprinkling of vinegar enhances the flavour. I realise that this will not appeal to the health-faddists, but I also enjoy the legendary chip butty, always prepared in thick slices of white bread coated on one side with margarine. The peas should be mushy and hot, of a consistency similar to that of the tuna described a few sentences earlier.

But on these sullen nights, with thunder belching in the sky, my memory drifts back to the streams of North Wales and the fisherman who advised me that it is unwise to make a big noise in life. People will see that you have caught a fish or hooked some other trophy. It is for them to judge whether you are worthy of the accolades. You are not measured by success, though it might carry its own rewards. Your true worth lies in what you can offer to others.

The musings of a Liverpool columnist

The great leveller

The incorrigible optimist pounds down the pavement, hand outstretched, his face polished with an over-dose of shaving lotion and never-say-die festive cheer, his evangelical grin as wide as split water melon.

"Greetings, old chap. Splendid to see you again. Now, tell me, what did you get for Christmas?" he asks, and passing through my eyes, still red-webbed by too many wee drams of John Barleycorn, I could see a squadron of answers to his question lining up on parade.

Socks, hankies, spray-on hair-restorative, a mosquito net, a wallet, gift tokens, surgical stockings, wart-remover, a complete guide to all the world's wars, a snorkel, photographs of Scunthorpe at the turn of the century, a fishing rod, an unabridged edition of the Book of Mormon, a chest expander, a jar of crystallised fruits, a reproduction-antique barometer, goggles, maroon underpants with hidden uplift for sagging buttocks, a pedometer, a good sex manual, a whoopee cushion, an electrical toothbrush, a butterfly net, executive-style shirts, weed killer for the gardener of all seasons, trousers with elasticated tops, a home-brewing kit, a book on how to enjoy an active retirement called *Hurry, While There's Still Time*, tartan slippers, an exercise bike, ice-blue new-man pyjamas, six ounces of pickled onions, a duck-whistle, an even-your-friends-won't-notice toupee and tips on how to shoot the rapids at Swat on the North West Frontier.

Instead, though, I answer the question with disarming honesty. "As it happens, I got gastroenteritis for Christmas. The strain placed on what are amusingly called my muscles when I was convulsing over the lavatory triggered off an attack of sciatica, which in turn caused painful spasms in my lumbar regions. What did you get?"

Now, I can almost hear you chortle – against your finer judgement, of course. In this country, for reasons deeply rooted in the national psyche, tummy upsets and back pain are treated as suitable subjects for fun, unless they are really serious, when the mood changes completely.

But the sound of vigorous flushing, coming as a prelude to the emergence of dad from the smallest room, his face the colour of an auld priest's vest and his innards squeezed like a lemon, is enough to delight the whole family.

"Vindaloo curry for supper, followed by treacle pudding and lumpy custard," his wife calls up the stairs, as perky as a milkmaid, swishing a bead of mirth from her cheek.

Perhaps gastric conditions amuse us because they remove all notions of class and position. The boss is no longer the boss when he is perched on porcelain, drops of perspiration squirting from his brow, winceyette pjamas at his ankles, clinging to his stomach, while moaning softly like a weary bee trapped in a jam jar. Diarrhoea rather than money is the great leveller.

Back pain, on the other hand is associated with malingering, traditionally in the armed services, though civilians have now caught up. This is because it is difficult to prove or disprove. When the comedienne says, "Ooh I'm a martyr to me back", you know what is meant straightaway.

Yes, there are conditions which can be diagnosed and treated effectively. But even doctors will admit that it is often difficult to know why one person's back should hurt so much and another's should be pain free. In such cases, painkillers, muscle-relaxants, rest and gentle exercise are usually prescribed.

Back to the bathroom.

In a cunning pincer movement, my gastroenteritis struck from one side as a severe cold advanced from the other. So, at the height of my discomfort, I was flowing enthusiastically from the nose, the bottom and the mouth. And, as you will have realised by now, I am a poorly co-ordinated fellow, never entirely confident about pedalling a bike and steering at the same time. Isn't life a tease?

Gender, of course, plays a big part in this. For various biological reasons, including giving birth to us, women claim to be much better than men at resisting pain and making light of illness. The evidence for this assertion, I have to say from personal experience, is rather slight. But like so much else of questionable veracity, it is widely accepted as the truth.

Anyway, there can be no disputing that on Boxing night, I was an undignified sight on the bed, whimpering and drawing up my legs with each spasm. From her vantage point at the other side of the bed, my wife described my symptoms to a nurse on the phone at the hospital's emergency out-of-hours service.

"It is difficult to tell how bad it is," she said, "because he's a man and you know what they're like."

This observation immediately sparked sympathetic ribaldry between them. I didn't have the chance to tell them that lifting weights, particularly from the shops and in the garden, is the major cause of back trouble among men.

Life, love and washing up

Hop, skip and jump

Just one word caused a sly, half-smile to ghost across my lips when the aluminium doors to one of the lifts to the upstairs wards at the hospital gasped opened.

"We'll jump on that one," said the loving husband to his wife, whose generous figure of some 13 stone was wrapped in a fluffy pink dressing-gown, from which a rubber-tipped crutch stretched to the lino floor from each arm-pit.

"Jump," I thought, here was the language of courage and unintentional humour springing out of miserable circumstances.

Even in her prime, when the thwack of hockey-sticks blushed her ears and mud splattered her awesome legs mottled by winter, I cannot imagine that this fine lady was ever a great one for the leaping.

But that is the way we speak, always mining the richest vocabulary in the world to colour the banality of our activities.

You may have noticed that Britons never walk to the shop or the pub. We pop, we skip, we dash, we zip, we hop, we zoom, we buzz, we spin, we trot, we race, we pad, we canter, we fly, we whizz, we might even 'mosey on down', if our childhood was influenced by cowboy comics. But we don't walk anywhere.

On a slightly different tack, an old friend of mine, who, as the expression has it, enjoyed a drink, once reprimanded me for suggesting that he had 'weaved' his way home. "I tottered," he said, with a certain indignation brushing his tone. "That is a gentler appreciation of my style of perambulation."

Hopping became my late mother's favoured mode of transport, after she had her second hip replacement. On one occasion, in what must have been an alarming sight for her fellow shoppers, I recall her speaking of how she 'hurdled' between the baker's and the greengrocer's, in a frantic effort to shave seconds off her schedule.

My colleagues at work are mostly 'poppers'. Like a parade of balloons in a pin factory, they pop to the sandwich bar for lunch.

But in my experience only bubble cars truly popped, driven forward defiantly by their little two-stroke engines, which trembled to explosions of increasing desperation as they negotiated the gradient of an unyielding hill.

Hordes of the elderly population, in cardigans and surgical support-stockings, find themselves skipping from place to place, while their rusting limbs creak out a geriatric chorus.

"Hello Gwladys, is that you? This is me here," trills Agnes on the phone. "Stan was wondering if you would like to skip down to the bingo with us. Oh, I am sorry. You're having your bunions scraped. Maybe another time, then. Must dash, the kettle's calling. *Tempus fugit*."

My young wife, by comparison, is an aviatrix, who conducts her telephone conversations between flights. "Lovely to speak to you again. Must fly, time and tide waits for no woman," she chirrups. "Be in touch soon."

Fizzy or bubbly were words that cub reporters on local papers invariably plucked from their vocabularies when describing some toothless old wreck in a bath-chair, who had just "celebrated" his 100th birthday party with a slap-up meal, a spirited medley of wartime favourites and a romantic circuit of the dance floor.

In conversation, we are choosing words which give the listener a mental picture of the event, rather than a factual account. So the girl who looks rather pallid after a bout of flu has a face like cold porridge. This is puzzling to the stranger, but provides a wonderful image for those familiar with the urban English complexion.

Staying the dogs of war

It's almost over now.

Next Monday the nation commemorates the 60th anniversary of VJ Day, which marked the end of the most terrible war in the history of our kind.

The men, those who survived, still call themselves the 'lucky' ones, as though they had been dealt a flush hand by some divine shuffler. Now, they are growing old, though in the smile of the mirror they may still see themselves as they were in the green of their days.

Straight, young limbs which once ran to the sun, are bent and slow. Nut-knuckled, long-veined hands tremble on the teacups and tears come too readily to eyes which were always dry, then. You didn't let the side down, even when the lump in your throat was swelling so hard. Irony stiffens the air. The old comrades ask about each other's health and they all say, "Mustn't grumble, how are you?".

Bravery, like cowardice, is eternal, but the tread of time is merciless. Nothing can stop it's advance. Of course, there will be other VE Days and other VJ Days. But this is the last opportunity for mass gatherings of those who were actually there.

In a society, which measures the importance of years in noughts, the next big anniversary will be the 70th. Some will still be here, but they will be very old – slowly leaving life to enter history, like the ghostly survivors of the mighty armies from the fields of Belgium and France in the Great War, who, until a few years ago, were seen with ribbons of medals and rugs on their knees at the Cenotaph on Armistice Day.

Two abiding memories arose from our victory over the Japanese. First, there were the PoWs, beaten and starving in the slave labour camps, and then there were the bombs dropped on Hiroshima and Nagasaki in the closing weeks of the war.

Philosophers said that we had lost our innocence with the development of the atomic 'bomb' because it could destroy the world. An image loomed in the popular imagination of a crazed politician with his finger poised on the red button, which would release the bomb, starting a war to destroy us all. We spoke of the 'mushroom cloud' which would envelop everything.

But we had lost our innocence long before that. Since the bow and arrow, man had been inventing weapons designed to kill as many people as possible as quickly as possible. America had the bomb, the USSR, Britain and France soon followed. The Iron Curtain, forecast by both Hitler and Churchill, divided the communist East from the democratic West. This was the world of my childhood. We called it the Cold War because the principal belligerents themselves did not directly engage each other in battle, knowing that to do so could result in annihilation. Politicians called it the balance of power and they loaded more and more nuclear weapons – bombs, missiles, submarines and God knows what else – on either side of the scales.

However, there were 'localised' wars in Korea, the Middle East, Africa, the Indian sub-continent, Vietnam. Dreadful new weapons could be tested in these distant fields of the Cold War. But the bomb remained aloof, the most malignant weapon in the world, whose very malignancy made it unusable.

In common with many of my generation, I joined demonstrations against this "bomb", which was always referred to in the singular. We sat on damp pavements with our placards, singing *We Shall Not Be Moved*. For years there was a slogan daubed on a rail bridge, near the old Cammell Laird shipyard in Birkenhead, where they had made nuclear submarines. It said, 'Build houses Not Polaris'.

Some of my friends sat in the lotus position and nibbled raw cabbage leaves, so great was their concern that we should not destroy the world. I took to wearing a denim cap and lumberjack shirts,

Life, love and washing up

so that everyone could see where I stood on this question of the bomb. I was against it. Those in favour of it were mad. Ban the Bomb.

Yet, with the passing of the years, I came to realise that the bomb had spared my generation of Britons from what is known as "conventional warfare" – shooting, stabbing, gassing, strangling, kicking, starving, bleeding, burning and drowning each other to death for some cause or other.

We have been so lucky, much luckier than those who survived the wars. For war is not the province of heroes only. Those faraway graveyards are filled by people who otherwise might have been us – the good, the bad, the funny, the bossy, the bloody stupid, the kind, the gallant, the cautious, the daring, the dull.

Then you see the old women at home with their cats, fingering photographs of sweethearts who will never turn grey and you know we have been sent a good hand by that hidden dealer. All we have to do is respect our world and our country, with all its strange ways, and remember with gratitude those who went before. They wanted us to be happy for them.

⌣

Touring death

The bearded man, whose hair blew to the whims of the breeze, was dressed in jeans and a pullover of beatnik-black.

This was not the bearing of a military man. Here, I thought, was an admirer of flowers, who has read the words of philosophers and poets through his thick-lensed glasses in the smoke of cafes where dreamers smile.

One sandal-led foot was on the cobbles and the other rested on the lower pedal of his bicycle, as the men in tartan marched to the skirl of their pipes and the ancient rhythm of the drums, charging the blood of patriots with spurts of emotion.

And when they passed his place in the second row of the crowd, the man with the bike raised his fist in the modern salute and called to the disappearing soldiers, "Thank you, thank you, from the bottom of my heart, I thank you".

The back of his throat was dry with the passion which bring tears to your eyes, but his sentiment carried in the air.

With that he rode away from the Menin Gate in Ypres, the sad and strange place, where nightly, in a short service of remembrance, the hopes of today are chilled by all the lost tomorrows found in the 54,896 names inscribed in the walls. These are the men from Britain and her old Empire killed around this town in Belgium in the Great War.

That is a fraction of the total dead. This empty tomb is dedicated only to the men whose bodies couldn't be found or re-pieced for burial. But their spirits are with us as much as those of the soldiers lying for eternity in the groves of white crosses and poppies.

Maybe five steps from the cyclist was a mini-coach advertising tours of the battle sites in the Ypres salient. "So death is now tourism," I said to my colleague Howard Davies, who was there to take photographs. Neither of us felt that this was necessarily wrong, though the idea settles uneasily in my mind.

But since the dawn of travel, people have wanted to see all the great places in the world. It is our world after all, given to us by God, and our leaders and the brilliant few have filled it with many sorrows and follies as well as triumphs. The rest of us muddle on.

We were staying in Ypres with old and new soldiers from the Liverpool Scottish, who were visiting the sites of battles along the French/Belgian border, where their forebears had fought.

It is extraordinary to sit, sipping a frothy coffee, nursing a hangover, enjoying the sun, beneath this colossal monument of death. But that is what has happened in the lovely stone town. You walk from the tobacconist to the greengrocer by way of the Menin Gate. It becomes as familiar as the ebb-tide at a fishing port.

But here there is deep respect for the living ones as well. They come in their thousands to pay homage to the strangers in stone, who could have been them, but for fate and her perpetual mysteries.

So the boys of the Liverpool Scottish in their kilts, their knees knobbled for action, raised a few glasses for old comrades and then they raised a few more for the living. Laughter followed and digs in the ribs came with the in-jokes known only to the soldiers. These are hard men with eyes that could make you tremble and fists that would make you fall. But they have an affection, one for the other.

We walked to the Bellewaarde Ridge, where an attack by the Liverpool Scottish bad been stopped by German machine guns with the loss of hundreds of lives. The thick grass was drying in the sun. Men yawned and stretched. A hen squawked and scraped at the dirt by a fence in front of a painted windmill. The peace was touchable, but on the edge of the forest you could see a white cross over the memorial.

These lanes are not walked by sophisticated continentals. They are for country folk used to scraping the cow dung from their boots while loaves bake in the oven

"Would you do it?" asked Davies. "Charge at the enemy guns, knowing there was little chance of survival?"

I shrugged my shoulders, fearing the truth lay in the silence of my answer. "I would do it to protect my family," he said. "But I don't know about this." He opened his hands towards the field in an expression of bemusement and shook his head.

But then you have to understand that the Liverpool Scottish sees itself as a family, widening its embrace to gather in all those associated with it. At the farewell dinner in the upstairs room of a restaurant in Ypres, you could sense the force of tradition which holds them all in fellowship and loyalty.

The piper arrived at an appointed moment, filled his lungs with enough wind to launch a fleet of balloons, played perfectly and then, in a single swallow, downed a dish of whisky, known as the quake. He kissed the quake's bottom and left the room. We clapped and thumped the table. Tradition feeds blind courage.

And in the morning the sun rises and the man on a bike rides again towards the Menin Gate.

〜

Lust lore

A report from the government-backed Economic and Social Research Council has found that women now lust after men as much as men traditionally lusted after women.

This is an alarming thought for a fellow who has innocently advanced through life without once having his bottom pinched by predatory fingers in a crowded lift.

But is it true?

As I sit at my desk writing this column in a aqua-blue Terylene and cotton mix shirt, beneath which the webbing of my string vest is clearly visible, are the gazes of nubile computer operatives secretly undressing me? Do the heart-shaped mouths of blonde sales executives drool when I reach into my hip pocket for a handkerchief, with which to check a minor eruption from the persistent boil which has taken root in my left nostril?

During the recent heat wave, when climbing the escalator from the tube station, with green steam belching from the sides of my suede moccasins, I had the strangest sensation that eyes were fixed like limpets to the gentle sway of my buttocks. Beads of anticipation tingled up and down my inner thighs. On reaching the top, however, I was confronted by a man of military bearing. "I think these fell from your back pocket," he said, handing me my return train tickets. I smiled in pathetic gratitude.

There was no point denying it. Here was the truth. I am 57 and nobody has ever lusted after me, and those years when I might have prompted lustful thoughts are disappearing as fast as hopes in a bingo hall.

Even in this age of female dominance, I do not expect glamorous women to sidle up to me at the bar and say, "I hope you don't mind me joining you, but I saw you were alone. May I recharge your glass? What's that? Oh, I didn't think they would do Albanian wine here."

Certain people excite lust. Others rely on different qualities. When I was a teenager, blind dates would sometimes be arranged by friends, so that you would have someone to escort to the next party. I should explain that the word 'friends' here is applied rather loosely.

Descriptive words would be used to stir your anticipatory juices — 'gorgeous, ravishing, the eyes of Audrey Hepburn and the figure of Brigitte Bardot', being fairly typical of the language of the time.

But there were expressions which chilled the soul before they had completed the journey from lips to ear-hole. These would usually detail the person's character while skipping around the thorny question of looks.

"She's loads and loads and loads of fun, nobody had more spirit than her on the hockey field. Actually, she had an aunty on her mother's side who spent some time in Mexico breaking-in wild stallions," they would tell you, encouragingly.

In these arrangements, a sense of humour was always judged adequate compensation for almost any physical disfigurement. "She'll have you laughing until your sides split," her friends would advise. "Wait until you've heard her impression of Anne Shelton. It has brought grown men to their knees."

"When she smiles, her whole faces lights up," I was once told of a girl, who, on being introduced to me, opened her mouth to reveal teeth-braces of such magnetic force that they could altered the flow of traffic on the M1. She could have been employed to blind people on the Damascus Road.

While on the subject of lust, some readers have been asking why my Aunty Gwladys never married. Well, this is not strictly true. She was married, briefly, to a certain Bartholomew Postlethwaite-Withers, an army major of dubious provenance, who claimed to have served in Lincolnshire during the war.

Although there was a physical attraction, and they succeeded in consummating their marriage at the third attempt in a boarding-house in Cleethorpes, observers said that their class differences had proved too much, with the major adamantly refusing to stop slurping tea from his saucer.

Those closer to the couple, though, said that the blame lay with her devotion to Joey, the pet pterodactyl, whom she keeps in a cage in her parlour.

"Either that pterodactyl goes or I go," barked the major one day after a particularly demanding round of golf. It was no contest. "Who's a pretty boy then?" said Aunty Gwladys, as the major shut the front door behind him. Joey preened.

I think on balance that it is better not to be the object of someone's lust. Affection is a stronger emotion. The trouble with lust is that the bits of you which are meant to attract it tend to sag and fade with the passing of the years. After that, what are you left with?

My wife, whose beauty is eternal, said when she first saw me that I made her laugh. If that was true then, it must be doubly true now. Kindness, tolerance and wisdom are other qualities which should last and prove far more important than mere lust.

But the occasional wolf-whistle might ease our days.

﹏

Travelling heavy

Those of us equipped with memories which can still canter back to thumb-sucking nights by the fireside, will remember the fable of the three bears, who return home to discover that a stranger has eaten up all their porridge.

But the real significance of the story, to us social commentators, whose ears prick to the nuances of political correctness, lies not in the temerity of Goldilocks, but in the distribution of the porridge.

Daddy Bear, you may recall, assumed as his right the big bowl without recourse to any discussion; mummy bear accepted the medium-sized bowl with a contented sigh, while uncomplaining baby bear knew straightaway that his was the small bowl.

This is not the world as we know it now.

Let us take as an example the oranges taken from the fruit bowl after family meals. Our seven year-old-son reaches for the largest without the slightest qualm; my wife picks the most perfectly shaped, as she believes that it is home to the sweetest juice, and I am left with the loser; the runt in the bag, the fruit nursing an unsightly bruise. There are many variations on this theme, embracing almost all areas of life where pleasure can be measured.

Anyway, last Monday, I arrived home late from work, after a two-mile trek up from the railway station. My feet were steaming like a tramp on a treadmill, sweat was spouting down the nape of my neck and my brain was wincing to raps from the hammers of anxiety, stress and accelerating hair-loss.

"Once you have trimmed the hedges, back and front, I have got something very special to show you in the bedroom. I know you will really like them," said my wife, wiggling provocatively down the hall, as I leant on the porch wall waiting for my breath to regain its normal rhythm.

Feeling somewhat refreshed after a gentle 20-minute session on the shears, I headed for the bedroom full of nervous anticipation.

"There they are," said my wife opening the palm of her hand and stretching out her arm like a singer introducing the band. Along the wall stood three suit-cases; a big one, a medium-sized one and a little one, because, like the bears, we are a family of three.

However, as the Jane Marples and Hercule Poirots among you might have realised already, there has been an important change since our happy nursery days. For, in this new pecking order, mummy has the big one, baby has the middle-sized one and daddy has the small one.

"These will do for our holiday," said my wife, stroking the handle of her suitcase, which has been fitted with wheels. Suddenly, I was filled with the unexpected thought that man invented the wheel so that women could keep their wardrobes with them while chasing herds of caribou over the frozen wastes. But the moment passed.

Since we booked a two-week cruise on the Danube for our first long holiday in more than 12 years of marriage (she doesn't count hiking on Snowdonia), my wife has been on a solo mission to clear the shelves of the fashion stores, arriving at one before dawn on a sales' day to head the fiercest squad of women seen since the Amazons defended Troy.

Something called colour co-ordination seems to be the key to much of this buying. At this stage, I should give you an example of the cunning behind this seemingly innocent concept. The conversation goes something like this.

"I think I'll just pop into town to buy a dress for the cruise. I have my eye on a nice peachy colour."

"All right," says I, speaking up a little to be heard against the mounting groans from the floorboards under the wardrobe.

About four hours later she returns, followed by a parade of stooped taxi-drivers carrying parcels up the path to the door.

"I thought you only wanted a dress," I protest.

"Yes," she replies, "but you have to be colour co-ordinated." So I needed matching shoes, stockings, under-clothes, blouse, polar-neck, bikini, face flannel, jacket, the complete works of Percy Bysshe Shelley in a tasteful cover, hat, handbag and parasol."

"And what's that coming down the road," I add, in a tone of increasing incredulity.

"Perhaps I should have told you about the car," she says. "But don't be cross-patch. That would spoil everything."

When I was a young man and roamed the roads free and wild, I packed all my holiday clothes in a rucksack to which I attached the tent and camping utensils. Then I could feel the wind playing through my hair. Now it has an unobstructed passage.

But when I arrive, panting, on that cruiser after rolling our cases up the gangway, I know to whom the eyes of the crew will first turn, as she casts the beautiful curves of her shadow into the moonlit water of the Danube. Gipsy violins swirl in the still air and everybody will be held in the turquoise smile of my wife's eyes.

What is this though? The ship is listing strongly to one end. "Man the lifeboats," shouts the captain.

$\backsim$

The tyranny of time

A drip emerged from the tip of my nose a few mornings ago and then hung there in a sullen manner, like a limp yo-yo, as I waited for the steam to whistle through the spout of the old kettle.

"Where do all our days go?" I muttered to myself bleakly, observing through the kitchen window our rabbit Jasper's easy, leisurely lollop towards a carrot, which was glowing like a beacon in the dawn murk around his bowl.

At that moment, a news item sprang from the wireless and squirmed its way through the thickets of hair in my ear-holes, finally reaching my consciousness.

A scientist – in itself a word to freeze your few remaining brains cells – was apparently working on a clock which would be accurate to a single second over a period of more than 30 million years.

"Now there's a chap who has never boiled an egg," I thought.

Anyway, there are 86,400 seconds in a day. That would seem to be a precise enough division of time for your average wallah working out a new timetable for the number nine bus.

Taxi drivers, of course, have their own unit for measuring the passage of time. It's called the jiffy. "Hold on there, mate, he'll be with you in a jiffy," says the jocular telephone-operator to the waiting customer, who wonders which will arrive first – the car, or notification that a bed is free for her hip replacement operation.

The line to supermarket check-out desks, too, provide us with a splendid opportunity for considering our own mortality and the growth pattern of warts.

To the gentle rhythm of ticking clocks, I close my eyes to think of the queue and I see glaciers blistering past it.

Anyway, it seems that the Phileas Fogg types at the National Physical Laboratory in London were not satisfied by our present system of timing. So, they are working night and day to make a more accurate clock, involving the bombardment of strontium iron with optical-frequency light.

The current method of measuring time employs caesium atoms absorbing microwave energy. But it loses one second in every 30 million years, which, quite simply, is not good enough if you want to impress the boss.

As all this was being explained on the wireless, my mind wandered back to a downy-skinned, sunny afternoon in the mid-1950s, when I had bought a book about good, God-fearing King Alfred, who was by nature a punctual fellow – so much so that he invented his own clock.

There was a picture of him with a lit candle which had rings around it. Each time the melting wax reached a lower ring, you knew that an hour had gone. This must have been such a boon when arranging fixtures with the Vikings' mighty warlord, Guthrum.

I imagined them in a tent. "Our armies shall meet in bloody battle at Athelney Marshes when the wax reaches the third line," said Alfred, "and we shall call it a three o' clock kick-off."

From then on, they synchronised candles and, in most ways, this was a splendid indoor clock.

However, it was susceptible to gusts of wind, rather like my dear Aunty Gwladys, after a surfeit of sprouts. You could, of course, shelter your candle in a lamp. But, I fear, this would have been rather impractical if you were joining the hurly-burly of commuters, sprinting, elbows out and coats-a-flap, for the station to catch the 6.32 train to Bootle.

"Excuse me now, sir, sorry to delay you, but could you tell me the time? Careful, there, don't look too closely, or you'll scorch your eyeball. Oh dearie me, it's gone out. Isn't that our luck? Don't be like that. Your other eye still works."

Life, love and washing up

What really concerns me about this zippy new clock is how we are going to test its accuracy. Even those fit people, who pump iron in the gym every day and jog at the weekends are unlikely to be around in 30 million years, checking their watches for that errant second.

Have you noticed how long it takes for a drip to fall from the nose of a man suffering from the winter snuffles? It feels like an eternity.

I broke from my reverie to look outside the kitchen window. Jasper was finishing his brilliant carrot. He raised his head, sniffed the air and twitched his whiskers. The kettle was whistling and beyond the river the sun was rising. Pips sounded for the seven o' clock news on the wireless. Bread was toasting under the grill. You could hear the metal shutters opening on the shop across the road. My wife sighed deeply on her pillow, dreaming of our forthcoming wedding anniversary – 13 years together. Then the wicked alarm bell rang as rude as a cockerel in a yard, slicing through her warm thoughts.

Yes, all is measured by time, even those things which are precious to us. It's the tyrant you can't smell, touch, see, prick or taste. It always wins. You can never gain time, but you lose it, all the time.

Jasper yawned and stretched. Time will never be his master, for he doesn't watch its passing.

〜

Compassion

It was a peculiarly English scene at the little railway station which serves a seaside town.

The train juddered to a stop and a stooped figure advanced from the sheltered bench with unsure steps. His open anorak was bleeding puffs of padding and his body arched to one side, supported by a walking stick. Bulging the pocket on the other side was a can, which aficiandos of such matters would have spotted from the label peeping out, contained an alarmingly potent brew of lager.

Following a few ginger steps behind was a perjink figure, in a sports jacket and crisply pressed twills, almost set in sepia. A paper was folded under his arm and there was a look of recent retirement in his bearing – maybe he had been the under manager in a minor branch of a small bank, who now keeps meticulous minutes for the Rotary Club. Grey dashed the parted hair, clinging to his scalp with a determination which would have defied the ruffling of the breeze on the golf links. This was a decent and kindly man, I thought.

The train was sparsely filled, the broken drinker collapsed onto his seat and took a long swig from his can and belched, before sinking into a deep sleep. Discretion had persuaded the other man to sit a few rows away, where his eyes studiously avoided the slumped figure.

Then steam began rising from the drinker's lap and his fawn trousers darkened around the thighs and crotch. Although every eye now was barnacled to the windows, following the passing landscape, we had all noticed. But the drinker slept on.

What should we have done? Such situations worry the private and suburban sensibilities of the Briton. I had seen this drinker many times at railway stations, always begging for money. Usually, I have given him something towards his next can or bottle. I respect his honesty, his direct manner and understand his ceaseless thirst. He has no act, no subterfuge about needing a few coins for his fare or a meal. He just asks you straight for money, no frills.

Someone on the train could have woken him and made some futile enquiries about his heath. We could have told a guard about his distressed state. We could even have offered him the money for a pair of new trousers, but I fear that his instinct would have guided him to the off-licence. But, this being England, we did nothing at all, leaving the train at our respective stations, as the poor chap slipped further into the brief comfort of his oblivion.

At first, you might feel that we were neglectful of a fellow human and, to be sure, he will be in need of formal help soon and that will end his freedom, such as it is. However, I believe that on this suburban run, on a gloomy, English day, we were not demonstrating our indifference to the misery of another, so much as a desire not to humiliate a man in the moment of a shame, which reaches back and back and grazes childhood memories in us all.

Life is not just a hammered thumb

Pessimism is as much part of my being as the bruise on a picture-hanger's thumb.

From the first blinking light of the pillow-puffed morning to the spill of cocoa on my pyjama jacket in the creeping dark, I fear that life's hammer will be waiting, a-rap-tap-tapping, around the next corner.

Some people call this condition depression, but for me it is just the sensible anticipation that the fellow kneeling on the hassock immediately in front of your pew in church will have recently stepped on a hillock of dog dirt, cunningly disguised in the russet leaves heaped along the pavement as an invigorating herald of winter.

This mood deepened last Monday when a friend and colleague turned 48, celebrating the occasion by releasing the top button on his mauve shirt with a devil-may-care flourish and a barely audible wheeze, before treating us all to a little hop in front of his desk.

"Almost 50 now," I said to him in cheery tones, as a flash of pain leapt from his left foot to his rheumy old eyes.

"No, 48," he snapped back, prising a drawing pin from the thin sole of his Italian-style shoes. "Still two years to go before the big Five-O."

"Mmmm," I said, sympathetically. "Of course, you will find that the years start whizzing by now that you've entered what we call the home run. Soon, you will start looking along your book shelves, wondering if there will be time to read them all before that trumpet blasts in the sky. And then you'll have to accustom yourself to the quirks of people. For example, you will never be quite sure whether the bank manager is shaking your hand or feeling your pulse. They have to take precautions, you know, part of the job. Still there are compensations. Heavily pregnant women will offer you their seats on the bus and friends will forgive you for forgetting their names.

"What's that you say? No, no, I don't think your wife will, but there are certain tricks for remembering girls' names. Give yourself a little mental test every morning when you're brushing your teeth. Sorry, I didn't realise they weren't your own."

I don't find the English pessimistic by nature, but my background is mainly Scottish with a pinch of Irish sprinkled into the mix. This, I am told by experts on such matters, is a recipe for gloom. Worse than that, though, I have spent the majority of my summer holidays in North Wales, where they think that more than three shades of grey in the sky is a rainbow.

But I am positively throbbing with hope compared to an old friend, who used to slump in his great coat on a stool by the bar in the local pub, scratching the back of his hand on his grizzled chin. Rumours, whispered over the lino tiles, suggested that he had been a professional boxer earlier in his career and that might have altered his outlook as much as it had his face.

He was very witty, as you would expect from such a person, but this was the humour of the gallows and it was never well received, or even understood, by the numerous young ladies whom he had yearned to hook with his appreciation of World War One poetry. They preferred Paul McCartney to Wilfred Owen and really that was that.

Last time I heard of him he was digging holes for the Gas Board to finance the writing of his poems and short stores. I fear that few of these will have been published, but I am sure they are masterpieces of melancholy just the same. His holes, too, were probably masterpieces of their kind.

As I say, although some of these qualities are found in the English, their nature seems generally to be more robust than that of the Celt. A couple of weeks back, I was standing on the squelching touchline of one of the many football pitches laid out on a huge field, watching our son keeping goal, when a battery-operated invalid tricycle came wobbling over a crest.

At the handle-bars was a doughty matron, whirring through the mud in her overcoat and muffler, imperiously ignoring the rain as she rolled on, past the games and the bellowing crowds, touching fully 3mph on the open stretches.

I watched her disappear into the distance, thinking that she embodied much that is fine in England: the conquering of adversity, the defiance, the indifference to fashion and the thick-boned determination.

By comparison, I recently received an email from advertising consultants, who addressed me in the following way: "False eyelashes are big this season! In true style, trend-setter Madonna (apparently a dancer and singer in the popular mode) has gone one step further by opening the MTV Europe Awards 2005 in Lisbon with eyelashes encrusted with £20,000 worth of diamonds!"

During a moment of fantasy, I began thinking about the present I will buy my wife for our wedding anniversary later this month. But a nice painting for the wall would be better, which brings us back to hammers and thumbs.

⌒

Hair Today ...

The sight of an empty shampoo bottle skulking by the tub of ear-buds in the bathroom cabinet no longer casts me into the realms of darkest misery, as it would have done in the days of my ignorance.

For though not a scientist by calling, having never cartwheeled with delight to the fizz of chemicals in a tube, or indeed anything else, I have discovered a method of prolonging the potency of shampoo.

If you push a dent in the squeezy bottle and then lower its squirter into the basin, it will suck-up water, orchestrated by a vulgar rasp of the sort, whose sudden and zestful release would be deemed an infelicitous accompaniment to the satin-lined coffin of the council's solemnly-gartered chief executive, as it passes your pew in church.

The water, in its turn, persuades the residue of shampoo in the bottle to froth again. This, sadly, cannot be repeated indefinitely. Eventually, the bottle will gust and gush its rude noises, but defiantly refuse to bubble. This is not unlike the dispiriting experience of the company accountant endeavouring to wring a third turn from the same teabag.

I was thinking of these matters, as I watched a hair, formerly of my head, clinging tenaciously to the rim of the plughole. "Goodbye old friend," I whispered, as it finally succumbed, before adding, more emotionally, "farewell companion".

And so it was that I arrived in the chemist's shop. "What do you want?" asked the assistant in that enchanting way of today's people.

I was reminded of those times, a generation ago, when the pigeon-toed young man would appear at the same counter, anxious to buy condoms with which to satisfy the demands of his strapping girlfriend, the pink-thighed, pickle-sucking centreback in the local hockey team, whose pantaloons could have rigged a medium-sized schooner.

"How can we help you, sir?" the assistant would ask with a crafty smile, as the pimples switched on and off across the rubicund countenance of our young man. "Is it more cough drops, you are needing?"

"Yes, that's it," he wheezed, twisting his legs. "More cough drops, please."

"That seems to be a very persistent cough, you have, sir," continues the assistant. "You must have been taking the drops for several months. There wouldn't be anything else I could be getting for you now, would there?"

"No, thank you, the cough-drops will suffice," he sighed, his head drooping again.

Anyway, back to the shampoo. These days I feel slightly vain even asking for it, given that it will hardly have to sweat, cleaning my remaining hairs. A lawn-mower in the tundra would find life more labour intensive.

The assistant placed before me an orange bottle described as a creamy fresh shampoo with soy milk proteins and succulent and scrumptious peach extracts. "Do you think, I'll really need that?" I asked. "It sounds more like a soufflé."

Before the answer came, I read further down the label to a line which said, "For frizzy and unmanageable hair". Well, I can accept "frizzy". After all I live in a wet climate. Reliable reports have been circulating of garden gnomes drowning on the lower-lying lawns of our village, where a boat in the drive is a precaution not an affectation.

Life, love and washing up

But I fail to see how my few hairs could be "unmanageable", though we do have memories of Bobby Charlton, in the twilight of his career, charging down the football field with five golden strands, flapping over the polished dome of his head, from a parting set somewhere down in New Zealand's South Island.

In fact, I blame football for the frizzy condition of my hair. It's the inevitable consequence of spending hours every weekend standing on the touchline watching our nine-year-old son playing in goal.

And he gave us a fine performance in his team's 4–1 win, for which he was made man of the match. I can't remember seeing him so happy or proud. This was not the nonchalant shrug affected by a cool kid to whom everything comes naturally. He truly celebrated his moment and I felt the surge of his triumph, standing there is the squelching mud, watching and clapping, tears rising like a flood behind my eyes.

Then my imagination travelled back 50 years to a grey day in Belfast. Two men in cloth caps are rubbing their chins and watching the boys on the field. In the distance you can hear the keen ring of a bell as the pub door shuts. One says to the other: "Aye, you've got yourself a grand wee footballer there now, Mr Best. He goes past the others like a ghost in a crowd. You know, I wouldn't be surprised to see young George playing for a big club, one of these days."

Well, that's the way it goes. You can have the sweetest success, but nothing in life is permanent except the memories you leave for others. Still, if you're in an optimistic mood, why not squeeze the empty bottle a few more times and see if you can suck-up another triumph.

⌢

Holiday friends

A girl and two fair boys were sitting on top of a gate on a day when no cloud would dare invade the blue of a sky, where the sun, deep and orange like the yolk of a poached egg, was darkening their virgin-summer legs on the places not already covered by mud or pimpled-white by stinging nettles.

It was one of those iron gates with ancient wheezes in its hinges, which shuddered and clattered when the smaller bit was fastened to the larger bit by one of those handles which you lower into a rusted groove.

In their hands the trio, now quite inseparable, carried apple slices and carrots. The brown-haired girl was nine, two years older then the boys. Perhaps because of this, she seemed to be in charge, adopting a slightly maternal attitude towards her two young friends, who periodically kicked the warm, humming air, as they wondered whether the ferns rooted on either side of the gate should be fashioned into deadly spears.

But for the moment the focus of six steadily staring eyes was on a magnificent chestnut horse, grazing and occasionally snorting behind several clumps of gorse.

The children had made his acquaintance briefly the previous evening, when steaming off the last of their energy on the narrow lane of crusting cowpats, which rises and twists steeply from the horse's field. At this meeting the horse had been pleased to see them, galloping from the far end of the field to the gate, before which his great hooves crushed little slabs of slate while he dipped his mane into their stroking hands.

Without recourse to debate, they decided that they would return the following morning carrying apples for their gentle friend with the sad eyes and the piano-key teeth. So there they were sitting on the gate, calling at the horse, whom they had named Benji for reasons dreamed in their imaginations. Now, those of you with long memories will remember how to the mind of a child the addition of a 'y' can transform a dull word, which would otherwise limp along in a sentence, into something that sparkles and immediately promises laughter or emotion.

"Food, Benji, food over here," they called together, pointing at the bags of rosy apples. Benji was disdainful, flicking his tail at errant flies and grazing studiously in the opposite direction.

And then the Welsh girl, who was sitting between the boys like mother on this day, shouted in a hillside soprano, which would have pierced the ears of any eisteddfod judges lurking in the vicinity,

"Foody, Benji, foody over here!" Soon they were all calling "foody". The magic worked and the horse turned to examine his greeters and then he trotted over, dignity satisfied by his leisurely advance.

But, as I watched from the other side of this lane under a haze of floating heat, I could see that the horse, despite himself, enjoyed his apples, picking them in preference to the carrots.

I had taken my son camping in his auntie's garden in one of the heather-tufted fields surrounded by rough-stone walls which are such a feature of the country around Snowdon. Within minutes of our arrival, he had developed a friendship with the girl next door and her cousin in the house next to that. At this age children sense the proximity of creatures similar to themselves with the skill of wasps sucking jam from toast.

After the introductions, which had been completed after some preliminary hurdling of the fences between the houses, they were off. It was one of those perfect weeks. To adults they are lost in the hope-shrinking return to work and all those decisions and meetings which we like to think are part of the 'real world'. But to children they remain forever warm in the memory, fresh as the blood spreading from a bramble scratch. Reluctantly they left the horse and began climbing the hill.

The conversation moved to cats. Would a cat be friendly with an elephant, the girl wanted to know. Would a cat be friendly with a lion, the other boy wanted to know. So it went down the scale until my son asked whether a cat would get on with a worm.

I had anticipated this decline and was ready with a reply. "The general answer is no," I said, "but there are exceptional cases. For example, Wimpole the worm and Sheridan the cat enjoyed a long and happy friendship based on their mutual interest in stamp-collecting."

I was rather proud of that response, though it was received with appreciative chuckles rather than the belly laughs I thought it deserved.

Anyway, the days drifted by in football matches, walks, climbs and iced lollies sucked dry on their sticks. Each dusk was met with long goodnights as the sands of the holiday slipped away. Friendships made between children on days like these are so strong and loyal.

Too soon, though, came the day of parting, with embarrassed goodbyes before my son finally waved from the back window of the car until his holiday friends were lost to his sight.

⤳

Deliver us from temptation

Sharp mouse eyes were watching the sleek cats of the prowling night, still padding and stretching and yawning, tails high, in the polished-stone alleys, as I left the house and strode into the chilled dawn towards the village shop, where the clatter of rolling metal shutters heralded the start of another day.

And lurking on the edge of a puddle outside the shop was a silver fifty pence piece, shining as bright as a prefect's badge.

Raising my collar, I squinted furtively up the two roads, which run on either side of the shop, to make sure that nobody could see my guilt, then I stooped to pluck the coin, feeling my hips creak and groan like an auld gate on rusty hinges.

I slipped the coin deep into the folds of a pocket on my corduroy jacket and regained my feet as quickly as age and arthritis allowed.

"Good Morning, David," said the keeper, emerging from the shop door, carrying a crate of cauliflowers to be laid on a table beneath the awning. "Did you drop something?"

The sun crawled up a black cloud to cast its rays across the scene and I blushed like a teenager spotted at the keyhole to the girls' changing-room.

The prayers, which had bruised my knees in young days, thundered again in my head and I could hear the flames of hell-fire cracking and cackling somewhere under the pavement.

"I have just found this," I said, producing the coin, "perhaps we should put it in one of the charity cans".

On the walk back to the house, I found my step agreeably refreshed. I had done something good for others. Although not generally of a theological inclination, I began to wonder in the thin air of coming day if the 50p would be enough to secure me a berth in Heaven, which I am told is even nicer than Lower Bebington when the crocuses are out.

The alternative is not a happy one. A fellow of a sensitive and poetic disposition shudders at the prospect of his delicately dimpled buttocks being roasted for all eternity on the hobs of hell, for the sake of a mere coin.

After all, these days 50p is insufficient to buy a cup of weak tea in the charity shop's cafe, located, as some of you may already know, behind the rows of second-hand coats, the stacks of surgical boots, the heaps of good-as-new pantaloons and briefs, and the table selling used copies of The People's Friend magazine.

As with most people of my generation, I believe that our good and bad deeds on earth are constantly being measured by some quality control operative. For example, if I accompany my wife to the supermarket, I would expect to soar within breathing distance of Sir Cliff Richard, way up there is the stratosphere; but should I sulk and fidget like a child when she is watching American comedy shows on the telly, I would expect to feel the devil's fingers tickling my feet. Your rating rises and falls through the tortuous journey of life.

Sunday mornings are a case in point. There we are lying in the bed, snug and warm, supremely comfortable, and feeling safe and protected, but the fingers on the clock are whizzing round as fast as they can to end our one lie-in of the week. Who should make the tea? That is the soul-stretching question.

In fact, the job involves rather more than brewing the tea. Our nine year-old son's breakfast has to be made and then there is the rabbit who has to be fed and watered and released from his shed at the bottom of the garden.

But on returning to our bed with the tray last Sunday, I found that my wife was wide awake and in religious mood, discussing the meats banned by people of various faiths.

"Did you know that the Jews do not eat pork and shellfish?" she said. "Muslims won't eat pork either, Hindus don't eat beef, Sikhs don't eat any meat at all. But Christians eat everything, apart from vegetarians."

"I am sure you could find a juicy, succulent vegetarian, if you really tried," I replied with a wicked smile. "The enjoyment of a dish always depends on the seasoning. That is where the French have us over a barrel, so to speak."

"Oh do shut-up," she said. "That is so typical of you, deliberately misinterpreting me, so that you can make a cheap joke. I have never known anyone laugh louder at his own jokes than you. Look at you now, you can hardly contain yourself and the tears are rolling down your cheeks and your tummy's wobbling like a jelly. Pull yourself together."

I suppose most of us do good and bad things, as our rating rise and fall along the way. On one side are the twinkling temptations and on the other the anticipated rewards.

Many smart young people of today seem to doubt the old certainties. The new priests are the scientists who have power over how and when we are born and how and when we die.

But the whole world would benefit if we all did good down here in the hope of a higher reward.

~

Tyrannised Rex

Saturday night was ghosting into Sunday morning as the bitter air stiffened the still water outside. In the distance the boys with beer on their breath and lustful ideas in their minds left the pub, hooting, bellowing and releasing phlegm with each tribal chant – all of them stumbling home for bed and recriminations, regrets, and sore heads to be nursed in the bright light of day.

I remembered it all so well from my past.

But now I was sitting on the sofa, alone, watching the pendulum on the clock swinging away the seconds, in that steady drip of our lives.

On the TV, though, they had back-tracked 65 millions years, give or take a tea break, to the times when the tyrannosaurus was king of all he surveyed. This, it should be said, was mostly evil-smelling, hissing bogs, rotting carcasses and vast stretches of wasteland, patrolled by creatures swollen with carrion.

Even a sweetly-scented estate agent, with a purple handkerchief, silk underwear and a battery of clichés, would have struggled to make it sound as attractive as the Lower Bebington of today.

It seems, however, that the world of palaeontology has been cast into its own murky waters by the assertion of a bush-whiskered, hippie-eyed American, who has been studying bones all his life, that t-rex was probably a scavenger, not a predator.

"Good Lord, there's a turn up for the books," I can hear the

Life, love and washing up

eminent professors whispering in the groves of academe. Down in the trendy bars, the beautiful young ladies sipping frothy coffee are seized by anticipation.

For it had always been assumed that old t-rex had to chase his breakfast, thundering along the ground as the tip of his tail swished 50ft behind his nose.

The evidence behind the new thinking could be found in the creature's surprisingly small arms, our man on the telly said.

Students of the subject know that after emerging from the primeval slime most predators grew two long arms. Here, it may not be uncharitable of us to think of the American President George Bush.

Of course, in the case of t-rex these judgements are comparative. A decent chap would not have counselled a close friend to engage one in a bout of arm wrestling on the bar at Ye Olde Jurassic Arms.

Anyway, various scientists were looking at a t-rex skeleton, reassembled in a museum. Perhaps, after all, he had been a scavenger they agreed, pointing at the beast's puny biceps and comparing them to his mighty jaw, lined with teeth of a size not seen since Esther Rantzen startled the audience on Michael Parkinson's chat show by singing a sentimental song to the traditional Irish tune, *She Moved Through the Fair*.

Can these chaps be certain of what happened 65 million years ago? I know there are sages and holy men in distant caves with memories of a misty age before Cliff Richard stalked the Earth. But I can't remember whether I switched off the hall light and my wife lives in perpetual fear of leaving the bathroom taps running.

As the clock advanced into Sunday, my imagination began wandering far into the future.

It is the year 4005. The scene is our house. Creepers cloak the walls. Toads yawn on the lawn. But some things are hauntingly familiar. In a revival of today's craze for naming people after places, the house is occupied by a couple called Wigan and Bootle, or Wiggy and Boo as they are affectionately known to their friends.

Wiggy is in the back garden, digging in the cabbage patch, while Boo varnishes her finger nails in the dinette. Suddenly he calls in a voice trembling with excitement. "I say, Boo, look! I've found some bones. I think they could belong to a human spine. Gosh, the poor chap must have been stooped with toil."

"Dig on, Wiggy," cries Boo from the window. "Put more muscle into it, you slacker!"

Seconds later, he unearths a Tranmere Rovers programme, perfectly preserved except for a trail of salt tears staining the front page.

"Maybe he was a practitioner of the ancient game of Association Football?" suggests Boo. "Do you remember our history lessons at school? Miss told us that grown men, some of them of above average intelligence, used to kick an inflated ball up and down a field watched by thousands of people. Can you believe it? Talk about primitive man!"

Sweat courses down Wiggy's weary face as he digs deeper into the soil. Suddenly his spade strikes another hard object which he pulls from the hole.

"It's a foot," he hollers. "What a find. Look at the toes, they're all bent and gnarled and the heel has been worn smooth by supporting heavy burdens. That could explain the poor chap's back. What do you think we have here, some sort of domestic servant?"

"No, when those bones are reassembled, we will have a perfect example of Shopping Man (*Homo Patientus*) from the 21st century," she said, her lovely smile somehow stretching back to another age.

↬

Life, love and washing up

"Dad, where do babies come from?"

Some people would argue, quite adamantly if you pressed the point, that your average human being is brighter than the average daddy-longlegs, or the crane-fly as they are known in entomological circles.

The important word here is 'average', which allows for the possibility that a perky and ambitious daddy-longlegs, hauling a fleet of letters after his name, could outshine the sort of slow-witted or complacent fellow you would expect to find on the lower rungs of the civil service or in a public relations consultancy.

Of course, in the more academic disciplines, such as trigonometry or the appreciation of Mongolian architecture, the human generally emerges more strongly. But there is one field where even a congenitally dull daddy-longlegs has the edge over us. I am taking ginger steps here towards the delicate subject of sex education.

In theory at least, to the casual observer, this is an activity in which it would appear that we have been blessed with most of the natural advantages. For example, the bottom on a daddy-longlegs ends where his head begins. We, by comparison, have vital and interesting bits between the thigh and the neck. Obviously, this is more true of some than others. Many middle regions do not prompt unbridled enthusiasm in the thoughts of the viewer. It is not unreasonable to note that I am not a thriller myself.

Anyway, without recourse to manuals with names like *The Joy of Sex* or smutty jokes behind the bike sheds, the daddy-longlegs goes about mating mummy-longlegs with enviable aplomb. While we were nervously fingering buttons on the back row of the Plaza, they were at it like rabbits.

The other morning our nine-year-old son came into our bedroom wearing his Tranmere Rovers pyjamas and a serious expression. "Where," he said, as I prised open my sleep-encrusted eyes, "do babies come from?"

"God," I replied at once, feeling a flush of blood colouring my face to the shade of the skin on a Dutch cheese. "That's all you need to know. God knew we wanted a baby and he gave us you."

"But how was I put into mum," he insisted.

"Go on, tell him," said my wife, who had raised her lovely head from the plump pillow. "It's the man's job, like trimming the hedge, lifting paving slabs and washing the dishes."

"Well," I said, cornered like a frog between two water rats, "you do a bit of this and a bit of that and Bob's your uncle and Fanny's your aunt, a little hanky-panky, and before you can say, 'Jack Frost', the world has another helpless mouth to feed. Is that comprehensive enough for you?"

"Oh, I see," he said, grinning, with the dance of an imp in his eyes. "I thought it had something to do with the man planting his seed in the woman. How do you do that?"

"My turn to make the tea," I said, sprinting from the room faster than Seb Coe chased his peerage. Then, pausing at the doorway, I added: "You know that seed. It's called the seed of love and it grew in mummy's tummy until it had a smile as wide as all the happiness in the world. When that happened you were born."

In my childhood, in the grey 1950s, when Corn Flakes were a treat, nobody ever mentioned sex, though occasional references were made to breeding or mating, which suggested that we were prize cattle or pedigree spaniels. I was left with the impression that there was a stud in the neighbourhood whose services were called on when required.

Otherwise passion was expressed in Jane Austen's novels and the occasional suggestive clue slipped into the old Daily Sketch's coffee-time crossword puzzle.

A little later, however, I noticed magazines in the shops which

Life, love and washing up

paraded girls in various stages of undress. One shop sold particularly bold magazines. Some of these were sealed for the delectation of certain clients, who ghosted in during their lunch breaks at the bank or the insurance office and left with a magazine or two concealed in their brief-cases, so that they wouldn't be spotted by fellow members of the parish's organ restoration appeal committee.

My great interest at the time was the Wild West and this was the only shop in town that stocked the pulp magazines, which described in impressive detail the battles fought between the Red Men and the cavalry. Regulars would wink at the counter assistant in a cunning way and point at publications with names such as Nuns on the Razzle, while, in my schoolboy treble, I asked if he had the November number of True West.

Now everybody talks about sex. You can't cloak your child in innocence. Last weekend, I noticed condoms strewn across the field, beneath the old quarry, where I play football with my son. My fervent hope was that he would not choose one as a goal-marker.

"Where do babies come from, dad?"

"They come from love, son, and your belief that life is precious. One day, you'll kiss a girl and then you will know."

꒰꒱

Man vs Underpants

The man, whose joints have stiffened to the cruel beat of the clock, knows that the chief difficulty in pulling up his underpants in the chill of morning comes with the second leg.

You stand there, with your porridge-grey Y-fronts held just above knee level, and gauge your left leg's capacity for upward thrust, while listening to the Prime Minister on the wireless waffling about how the dynamic new Britain is on the move. Be of good cheer.

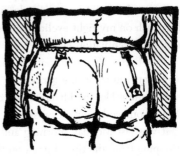

Harnessing your balletic skills to an enviable command of concentration, you raise the foot to the perimeter of the elastic belt and angle it over the appropriate hole, hop about a bit to prime all your muscles and limbs and then, with a single downward motion, you're home.

At this juncture, the optimist may see himself – puffing there in his string vest and bed socks, buttocks aglow before the bathroom door – to be a supreme figure of man, Michelangelo's statue of David made flesh, with a few creaks, creases and sags to add some earthly character.

But the celebration is of brief duration. Your wife sweeps open the door, demanding to know whether you have fed the rabbit yet. Lacking the co-ordination necessary to think and grip elastic at the same time, you loose control, allowing the underpants to slip down to your ankles, one foot in and one foot out.

The seasoned campaigner's solution to this dilemma is to lie on his

Life, love and washing up

back with both feet in the air and hope that the underpants will slide down the left leg to the point at which it is possible to bend the other knee and aim its foot into the empty hole.

This accomplished, you can smile at the day, confident that you have conquered its most daunting challenge.

"Bravo," shouts my wife, mopping a mirthful tear from her cheek, as I regain an upright position. "Have you considered yoga? People of your age need to remain supple or you'll seize up altogether. Everyone has a weakness, you know. For example, I have a recalcitrant lash on my right eyelid. You, of course, have the will-power of a moth in ventilation fan.

"But bones are your main weakness. Even when you slip away from your duties in the garden for a sly gin, I can hear you clicking and grinding like the lift-hoist in a colliery. By the way, are you still taking your cod liver oil capsules?"

It was last Monday morning and the melting frost formed beads, drooping from the tips of grass on the lawn, where our rabbit Jasper sat, already satiated.

On the best of weeks, Mondays have a melancholy glower. But this time it was worse. In addition to the struggle with the underpants, I noticed that the belt on my trousers wouldn't fasten to the usual notch or even the one next to it, unless I sucked in like some Californian beach pensioner posing for a camera.

The problem was caused by the gluttony of the previous day,

 which had left my tummy as swollen as a footballer's wallet.

We have discovered a Chinese restaurant with a Sunday buffet, where for £6 an adult can eat as much as he likes. It's £3 charge for children. Among the dishes on offer are soup, spare ribs, prawn toasties, chicken thighs, kebabs, pork won tons, spring rolls, curried meats, fried rice, chow mein, vegetables, chips, fruit salad, jelly and sponge pudding.

Maybe it's because I was born in the years of post-war rationing that I like to eat my fill. Some years ago I was told by one of those naturalists, who wear green coats, wellies and deer-stalker hats and spend their weekends lying on their bellies with binoculars, that given the chance a toad will eat until he bursts – rather like the glutton in the famous Monty Python sketch, who sprays his innards around a restaurant after completing his last feast with a waifer-thin mint.

A more probable explanation for such behaviour is that leisure has become so precious in these days of increased stress at work, almost everywhere, that people seek to pack the weekend with as many pleasurable experiences as possible.

Still, I have done enough banqueting for a while. But it had been my son's ninth birthday, so we thought a treat was in order.

To me, nine is the last year of true childhood, when the happiness is there to feel like treacle in the soul and you can run and kick and wrestle. Every scab on the knee is a trophy worth more than a tick in an exercise book or a badge on your lapel and the only good girls blow bubbles with their gum.

It is a crazy time when your muscles swell and your heart beats ever faster at the promise of new tomorrows. So you dress in the blink of an eye and you don't notice that your socks are odd and that your hair is waving in tufts on the crown of your head.

To be nine is to be eternal. You would never have dreamed then that one day you would struggle and laugh at yourself in the mirror – pulling up underpants. Stay forever young.

⌐